P9-CCI-304

© Brett Patterson

About the Author

DAVID WOLMAN is the author of *A Left-Hand Turn Around the World* and writes for magazines such as *Wired, Newsweek, Outside, National Geographic Traveler,* and *New Scientist.* He lives in Portland, Oregon.

⊛ Smithsonian Books

HARPER

NEW YORK · LONDON · TORONTO · SYDNEY

RIGHTING *the* MOTHER TONGUE

FROM OLDE ENGLISH TO EMAIL,
the Tangled Story of English Spelling

DAVID WOLMAN

HARPER

A hardcover edition of this book was published in 2008 by Collins.

RIGHTING THE MOTHER TONGUE. Copyright © 2008 by David Wolman. All rights reserved. Printed in the United States of America. No part of this book may be used or reproduced in any manner whatsoever without written permission except in the case of brief quotations embodied in critical articles and reviews. For information address HarperCollins Publishers, 10 East 53rd Street, New York, NY 10022.

HarperCollins books may be purchased for educational, business, or sales promotional use. For information please write: Special Markets Department, HarperCollins Publishers, 10 East 53rd Street, New York, NY 10022.

FIRST HARPER PAPERBACK PUBLISHED 2010.

Designed by Nicola Ferguson

The Library of Congress has catalogued the hardcover edition as follows:

Wolman, David
    Righting the mother tongue : from Olde English to email, the tangled story of English spelling / David Wolman. — 1st ed.
        p. cm.
    ISBN-13: 978-0-06-136925-4
    ISBN-10: 0-06-136925-X
1. English language—Orthography and spelling—History. I. Title.
    PE1141.W65   2008
    421'.52—dc22   2008023424

ISBN 978-0-06-136926-1 (pbk.)

10 11 12 13 14   OV/RRD   10 9 8 7 6 5 4 3 2 1

For Mom and Pop

I would advise you not to consult geese in matters of spelling.

—E. B. White, *Charlotte's Web*

CONTENTS

ONE

WAR OF THE WORDS

"There is no excuse, however, for 'thru' for through from any point of view."

Benjamin Ide Wheeler, September 15, 1906[1]

THE STUDENTS IN STANFORD University's "Calamity Class" of 1906 must have thought the world was falling apart. Five months before graduation, the Great Earthquake leveled much of San Francisco. More than 3,000 people perished, and the destruction and subsequent fires left some 225,000 residents homeless. Overseas, Italy's Mount Vesuvius had just erupted, again. Russia was recovering from a revolution and war with Japan. A tsunami in Hong Kong and earthquakes in Ecuador and India had killed tens of thousands of people.

The United States was not engaged in military conflict at the time, but the Spanish-American War was fresh in the collective memory. On the other side of the Atlantic, Europeans were planting the seeds of political foment that would lead to World War I, and, closer to home, Upton Sinclair's muckraking exposé, *The Jungle*, was shocking readers with its grisly portrayal of working conditions in America's turn-of-the-century stockyards.

Thirty miles to the south of the devastated City by the Bay, the earthquake had caused considerable, although less catastrophic, damage on the Stanford campus. Still, the graduates of 1906 had been dubbed the "Calamity Class." Their four years at Stanford were marred by a trio of campus tragedies: A typhoid epidemic in 1903, the death of Mrs. Stanford in 1905, followed by the Great Earthquake. They finally celebrated graduation on September 15, 1906.[2]

It was a typically sunny day on campus when Benjamin Ide Wheeler began his commencement address. Wheeler, president of the University of California and a renowned language expert, opened his speech by commenting on the recent destruction wrought by nature, and humanity's inherent resourcefulness and generosity in times of adversity. But then he turned to a battle that was gripping the nation. A rebellion was building momentum and Wheeler wanted it quashed. If the revolutionaries triumphed, he warned, the outcome promised "loss and waste to intercourse and culture."

America was at war over words. The composition of words, to be precise—what some people call orthography and the rest of us call spelling.* In its rise from a motley collection of Germanic tongues crossbred with French and Latin, spiced up by languages the world over and then churned through the lexicographic contortion machine of history, English, already on its way to becoming the lingua franca, had developed a nasty not-so-secret secret: its spelling system was a mess.

Amidst the thicket of foreign words, silent letters, and rule exceptions of English spelling lies more order than some people might

---

*Although spelling is a decent synonym for orthography, the technical definition of orthography is the entire writing system of a language, including not just spelling but also punctuation and capitalization.

expect, and likewise more chaos than others would like to admit. But when measured by the commonsense yardstick of consistent sound-to-letter correspondence, there's no denying that English spelling is a nightmare. Compared to the likes of German, Spanish, Italian, Finnish, and many other languages, our orthography is, as one scholar puts it, "flamboyantly inconsistent."[3] *Renaissance, millennium, diarrhea, bulletin, camaraderie, accommodation, feign, entrepreneur, rhythm, miscellaneous, cemetery, yacht, fluorescent, temperamental, license, perseverance, misspelling*—do any of these words ring bells of confusion? Not even *occasionally*?

As native speakers and readers, we rarely, if ever, stop to consider that the sound commonly represented by the letters *sh*, as in *shine*, is the same sound in *sugar, emotion, omniscience, charade, social*, and *fissure*.[4] Imagine the bewildered look on the faces of people learning English as a second language when they first hear about these *sh* shenanigans, or when the teacher writes out *rough, dough, bough,* and *through* on the blackboard, and then says that each is pronounced differently. These are quick examples, but they get right to the point, as do silent letters like the *g* in *gnarly* and the *k* in *knuckle*, inconsistencies like *mask* versus *masquerade* and *fear* versus *interference*, and geographic variations like *program* and *honor* in the US, compared with *programme* and *honour* in England.

For nearly as long as English has had a relatively stable or "settled" spelling system, there have been people complaining about it and campaigning for change. They've wielded a variety of arguments: A more phonetic spelling system would return English to a purer form, improve literacy, make time for students to tackle other areas of study, and reduce printing and proofreading costs. One of the most energetic times in the history of spelling reform was the turn of the twentieth century. "Philologists Declare War on Cumbrous Spelling of English," reported the *New York Herald* on March 18, 1906.[5] "Spelling Campaign Praised as Today's Real Need: Simplified Spelling Reform is Indorsed by Leading Citizens," declared the *Chicago Evening Post*.[6]

As a professor of philology (the predecessor to today's historical linguistics), Wheeler was a certifiable lover of words and kept careful watch over news from the front lines of this escalating conflict. Still, a commencement address about spelling? It doesn't exactly carry the weight one usually associates with such occasions, especially for an audience that had been through so much.

But that's the thing: Spelling matters. In Wheeler's time, spelling reform was no obscure topic. Heavy hitters from politics, education, business, and art were lining up in support of spelling reform. The newly elected president, Theodore Roosevelt, was a proponent of a revision scheme known as simplified spelling. In 1906 he began using some of the three hundred novel spellings suggested by a group called the Simplified Spelling Board, including *dipt* for *dipped*, *rime* for *rhyme*, and *tho* for *though*. He ordered the Government Printing Office to apply the new spellings to all future materials, although the order was soon revoked.[7]

The Simplified Spelling Board was captained by the esteemed bookworm Melvil Dewey, inventor of the Dewey Decimal System for the classification of library books. Joining him on the board were such influential figures as Columbia University President Nicholas Murray Butler, Stanford University President David Starr Jordan, Supreme Court Justice David J. Brewer, and *Century Magazine* editor Richard Watson Gilder. Steel baron Andrew Carnegie provided financial backing for the campaign.

Other luminaries also wanted to take action against spelling's weird twists and turns. (*Weird* was spelled *wyrd* one thousand years ago.[8] So much for "*i* before *e*.") Mark Twain had commented on the absurdity of English spelling, and Huck Finn's resistance to being "sivilized" is perhaps one of the most memorable misspellings in American literature. Playwright George Bernard Shaw repeatedly railed against English orthographic conventions, which he saw as part and parcel of the "middle-class morality" satirized in *Pygmalion*. In the play, Shaw wrote words such as *show* and *you've* as "shew" and "youve," and he famously quipped that combining the sounds derived from the *gh* in *cough*, the *o* in *women*, and the *ti* in *nation* would allow a person to pronounce the word *ghoti* as "fish." Journalist H. L. Mencken would soon weigh in on the matter, buttressing a call for reform by reminding his readers that notables such as Charles Darwin, Lord Tennyson, Sir John Lubbock, and Sir J. A. H. Murray, editor of the *Oxford English Dictionary* (*OED*), were all in favor of some kind of orthographic adjustment.

Spelling reform could not be easily dismissed. Practicality wasn't a primary concern for the believers because it never crossed their minds that this undertaking might be unrealistic. The atmosphere of the day, while reeking of industrial pollution, was filled with a sense of can-do. On the language front, it had been only eighty years since Noah Webster completed his magnum opus: *An American Dictionary of the English Language.* Eager to distinguish the newly independent United States from what he saw as the too-close-for-comfort cultural grip that England exerted from afar, Webster successfully altered the spelling of hundreds of words. For Americans, *gaol* became *jail*, *publick* became *public*, *travelled* became *traveled*, *centre* became *center*, and *valour* became *valor*—all because of Webster's handiwork. If a Connecticut farm boy could grow up to produce such a comprehensive and scholarly product as a dictionary, and if men could dig a canal across the Isthmus of Panama, surely across-the-board modification of the spelling system was within the realm of possibility.

In his commencement address, Wheeler outlined his opposition to spelling reform. With invective, he argued that the stakes of this battle were unimaginably high. That he shared the stage that day with Stanford's president and Simplified Spelling Board member David Starr Jordan, added an element of tension to the ceremony, and underscored the sense of urgency with which Wheeler spoke:

> The English language is not the property of the United States, still less of its government; it is a precious possession of the English-speaking world, and the moral authority to interfere in its regulation must arise out of the entire body and not from a segment thereof . . . Any radical change such as, for instance, would be involved in phonetic writing, would have the effect of cutting us off from the language of Shakespeare and the English bible making this a semi-foreign idiom to be acquired by special study.
>
> The proposal gradually to introduce, through the co-operation of volunteers, a certain number of new spellings, and then, when these are well under way, presumably certain others, seems to promise an era of ghastly confusion in printing offices and in private orthography and heterography, as well as much irritation to readers' eyes and spirits.

Irritated spirits indeed. But what about those of us whose spirits are irritated by the difficulty of the current system? I doubt that many bad spellers are drawn to careers in philology or linguistics, which makes Wheeler's stance somewhat predictable, not to mention biased. He did take a moment in his speech to acknowledge that the English spelling code has its disadvantages, but Wheeler's

concession was minimal; he was not going to waste breath expressing sympathy for the other side.

Besides, how could a true man of letters not embrace English
spelling in all its organic and idiosyncratic glory? Orthography, and
irregular spellings in particular, retain the etymological fossils that
give words historical richness and poetic power, and in turn give
philologists something to do with their time. In contrast, one can't
help but wonder whether Stanford President Jordan, an ichthyolo-
gist by training, became so incurably irked by the rest of the world's
inability to correctly spell *ichthyology*, let alone pronounce it, that he
viewed spelling reform as a way to overcome this problem of professional identity. (Ichthyologists, by the way, study fish.)

That morning at Stanford one hundred years ago, Wheeler spoke
of what he perceived to be the hazards of a "private orthography"
spinning out of control and leading to catastrophic misunderstand-
ing. Yet spelling has always had a private element to it. Despite our
shared cultural heritage bequeathed by teachers, writers, poets, playwrights, and lexicographers, our understanding of a word's meaning is by definition uniquely our own because reading and writing
first happen inside our heads. The same is true for spelling. Even for
the spelling bee contestant onstage, spelling is, at first, a private enterprise, during which a person chooses on the fly whether to spell
a word this way or that.

Multiply those micromoments of word consideration and construction over a lifetime, and suddenly you get the impression that
dealing with spelling occupies a serious chunk of our waking lives.
Strangely, though, the letters and order of letters in words are not
things most of us, with the exception of lexicographers and spelling
bee enthusiasts, spend much time thinking about.

That may change. In the century since Theodore Roosevelt's

presidency, spelling rebels were forced underground, but they didn't give up completely. Today, while reformers struggle to overcome a fractious constituency and dispiriting odds, a spelling uprising may be brewing without them; a revolution ignited by innovations born on the very Silicon Valley campus where Wheeler issued his warning one hundred years ago. But to discern what's on the horizon for spelling, it will help to see where English orthography has been and learn what it's been thru.

WHEN I WAS growing up, spelling was a source of substantial frustration. In Mrs. Damp's fourth-grade class, students were assigned one of three spelling books: The best spellers had the red one, the middle-of-the-road spellers had the orange one, and the more challenged spellers, myself included, had the yellow one. The whole thing blindsided me. It was as if overnight I went from being just like everyone else, to being singled out as one of the dumb kids. Since when did everyone master the art of spelling? Where had I been when it happened and why was everyone putting so much stock in this particular skill?

That was in the early 1980s, and spelling bees were not yet a televised phenomenon. But I knew about them, and the pageantry surrounding the coronation of spelling wunderkind. How could I not? Those kids, and even my classmates with their red books, seemed to possess superhuman powers. It was the ease with which they performed spelling operations that I couldn't fathom. I was still wrestling with the *-le* ending of *paddle*, *handle*, and *maple*, compared to the *el* ending of *angel*, *camel*, and *shovel*, to say nothing of *angle*, *level*, and *sandal*. Toward the end of the spelling worksheets came the big-money words, like *different (Is it a-n-t or e-n-t? It sounds* the same either way!), *restaurant* (*That can't be right. Where's the* o *I'm hearing?*), and *license.* (*Please, Mrs. Damp: Confusing the* c *and* s *yet again is going to be the death of me. Just move on already, to the foods of ancient Mesopotamia or even long division. Anything but this.*) Then, as we wrapped up the day's spelling exercises, I would steal a glance at some of my classmates' red workbooks and see *encyclopedia, curriculum, courteous, extraterrestrial, interference,* and *xylophone,* written up near the top of the page. I was stunned. *Those are their easy words?*

The thing is that I couldn't, and still can't, see words in my head in high-def the way talented spellers can. When I see a decent-sized word for the first time, my brain doesn't dice it into digestible, conveniently remembered groups of letters. Instead, all at once, I see this lengthy horizontal blob, and for a nanosecond the word looks like a cross between *schadenfreude* and HTML code. At that instant, my spirits get smacked with the same panic felt back in grade school, watching brainier classmates effortlessly write *curriculum* and *interference* as if those words were as short and simple as *nerd* and *envy.*

The deepest psychological wounds were inflicted at home. My brother Dan has always had a head for spelling. He's the youngest of four children and my parents encouraged him, intentionally or otherwise, in ways that built self-confidence and inoculated him against developmental pitfalls usually reserved for the baby of the family. Put another way: Dan was a gifted childhood speller, our parents praised him for it, and that's all well and good.

Except that I was also in the room. At dinnertime in our home outside Boston, I dreaded the impromptu spelling quizzes. It was as if the warm air wafting up from rotisserie chicken, green beans, and mashed potatoes hit some kind of mnemonic tripwire, reminding my mother of spelling bees from her childhood. Or maybe she thought some lighthearted word challenges would be a fun way to hear about what we'd been learning in school. What followed was a nerve-racking kind of game show minus the prizes. It was a perfect way to celebrate Dan's spelling smarts, while simultaneously leveling the playing field of brotherly combat that, due to our age difference, was lopsided in my favor.

Mom would choose a word and ask me to spell it. If I got it wrong, and the words were just tough enough that I usually did, either because I didn't know them or because anxiety got the better of me, my mom would then turn to Dan for the correction. I'd be lying if I said I could recall specific words from that bygone era—it's amazing I haven't suppressed the memories entirely. But I bet some of them were the same words that would dog me today were it not for the marvel of spell-check: *unnecessary, torment, vengeance, guaranteed.*

Those experiences stung. I interpreted my trouble with spelling at home and at school as an indication that the uppermost echelons of achievement were beyond my reach. And the feeling persisted. College, graduate school, fancy fellowship—in the recesses of my mind lurked this quiet fear that if someone were to observe via hidden camera just how much I rely on spell-check, I'd be outed, publicly scorned, and required to forfeit my degrees.

Sometimes when I think about language, my thoughts drift to those questions used to kick-start conversations in summer-camp cabins or company retreat conference rooms. If you won twenty million dollars, what would you do with it? If you could go anywhere on earth, where would you go and who would you bring? One such question that has always stuck with me goes like this: If you could have a single superhuman power, what would it be and why? Flight, immortality, mind-reading—there are some enticing possibilities.

I would choose to be fluent in every language. This desire stems from the fact that I travel a lot and regret my foreign-language ineptitude. But this wish for Tower of Babel software coded into my brain may also be an offshoot of my spelling woes, and of what I once perceived—and what society has led me to perceive—to be a deficiency when it comes to communicating in my native tongue. Spelling and fluency are obviously different, but being the planet's ultimate communicator would go a long way to alleviate the insecurity that goes with being a crap speller.

Decades have passed since those spelling duels with my brother, and although poor spelling skills haunt me, they're no handicap. I suppose it's a testament to the importance of word usage over spelling acumen that a guy like me can make his living wielding words that he can't spell aloud. Yet from time to time I can't help but wonder whether spelling ability reflects, if only just a little, a person's grasp of language. The same thought sometimes occurs when a misspelling foils one of my attempts at what should have been an easy crossword puzzle, or when I ask a Scrabble opponent for a spelling clarification. What does it mean not to be a spelling wizard?

As a weak speller, I have some questions that need answering. Why does English have such a screwy spelling system, and who can be blamed for predicaments like the silent "h" in *rhubarb*, the dizzying doubles in *reconnaissance*, or the *e*-versus-*a* confusion of *calendar*? Yes, *colonel* derives from Italian. But etymology isn't everything. Why weren't words coming into English from other languages adjusted for more regular spelling? What happened during history's most intense episodes of spelling reform? How did memorization of correct spellings become a coveted attribute of the educated class, and what will happen to orthography in cyberspace?

This book is my journey into the past and future of English spelling. It's an everyman's review of how the words of our language acquired their current form, a study of the quest to change the spelling code, and an exploration of spelling convention and innovation in the digital age. To begin, I need to retrace the origins of our language and the early influences on modern spelling. That means a hop across the pond.

TWO

CROSSED

... an acquaintance with the Saxon language, the mother tongue of the English, has convinced me, that a careful revision of our present dictionaries is absolutely necessary to a correct knowledge of the language.[1]

From the preface to Noah Webster's
A Compendious Dictionary of the English Language *(1806)*

THROUGH THE DAWN MIST, I watched as the engines of the SeaFrance ferry churned the dark teal waters into foaming, chaotic pools. The brasseries, B-rate hotels, and massive cable factory at the French port of Calais weren't here fifteen centuries ago, but the autumn weather may have been similarly gray. It was from coastal points such as this where the ancestors of English departed continental Europe for the mysterious island across the sea.

The boat's decor is hybrid discotheque-lounge circa 1991: yellow light fixtures, circular purple tables with matching leather chairs, and a zebra-patterned carpet. Near me a British businessman read Ian McEwan, a Muslim woman spoke French into a mobile phone, and three middle-aged Scandinavian women sipped vending-machine coffees and chatted loudly. A posse of lanky German high-school students paced between the videogame arcade and the front of the ship.

Travelers en route to Britain 1,500 years ago spoke a number of different languages. They were members of ancient tribes: Angles and Saxons, but also Jutes and Frisians. It's impossible to know just how intelligible each group and subgroup found each other, but the dialects and languages they spoke were all part of what linguists call the Germanic family of languages. Looking even further back, the predecessor tongue to Germanic languages is known as Proto-Indo-European, probably spoken in and around the Baltic areas of Europe some five thousand to eight thousand years ago.[2] Over time, tribes and languages began splitting and expanding throughout the continent, and the commonality of those dialects is visible in modern-day English, German, and Dutch. Look, for example, at *hundred*, *Hundert* and *hundrede*, or *bear*, *Bär* and *bjorn*.

The westbound forefathers of English were not settling uncharted territory. Even before the Romans came to Britain—*Britannia* to them—two thousand years ago, Celts and other tribes had already settled much of the country. With the rise of Roman rule, the Celts were assimilated, subjugated, and pushed toward the periphery. But what goes around comes around, and by the fifth century, the Roman Empire was collapsing.

The first Germanic tribes began arriving at about the time the Romans were hightailing it out of Britain. The opportunistic mercenaries filled a power vacuum, allowing them to reap the spoils of the vacated empire and occupy much of the island's prime farmland.[3] Not that the Celts passively relinquished territory; battles and skirmishes between the Anglo-Saxons and Celts lasted for another century. The victors, if they can be called that, gradually succeeded in displacing the Celts, who settled in what we know today as Ireland,

Wales, and Scotland.[4] Throughout the sixth century, more Anglo-Saxon warrior travelers continued migrating across the Channel. Over the next five hundred to six hundred years, their potpourri of tongues would blend and morph into the dialects of the Anglo-Saxon language, more commonly known as Old English. Incidentally, the spelling *olde* isn't old at all. Attempting to mimic archaic English spellings, nineteenth-century advertisers stapled an *e* onto the end of *old*. The trick worked, so much so that later generations came to think of *olde* as a true Old English construction. (*Old* has taken many forms throughout the premodern history of the language—*alde, auld, awld, ole* and others, but never as *olde*.)[5]

Old English was the era of *Beowulf* and other Anglo-Saxon poetry. The writing doesn't look too familiar through twenty-first-century lenses, considering that six letters from the Old English alphabet have since been lost, and the major changes to the lexicon in subsequent centuries. Still, there's an echo of modern English. This is a snippet from a famous seventh-century text known as *Caedmon's Hymn*:

Nu sculon herigean heofonrices weard,
meotodes meahte and his modgeþanc,
weorc wuldorfæder, swa he wundra gehwæs,
ece drihten, or onstealde.
He ærest sceop eorðan bearnum
heofon to hrofe, halig scyppend;
þa middangeard moncynnes weard,
ece drihten, æfter teode
firum foldan, frea ælmihtig.

Now we must praise the keeper of the heavenly kingdom
The power of the Measurer and his mind-thoughts,

The work of the glory-father; as he, each of wonders,
the eternal Lord, established from the beginning.
He first shaped, for the children of men,
Heaven as a roof, the Holy Shaper,
Then middle-earth, man-kind's Guardian,
The eternal Lord, afterwards created,
The earth for men, the Lord Almighty.[6]

Within this language lies the DNA of modern English, in words like: *weorc* (work), *wundra* (wonders), *ærest* (first), *hrofe* (roof), and *middangeard* (middle-earth).

Journeying across the Channel, I pictured a small fleet of modern-day vessels, maybe six of them, carrying the Germanic warrior travelers who would take over Britain and spawn the English language. The Anglo-Saxons looked out of place in their fur skins, sitting in leather purple chairs and sipping stale espressos. Yet there they are: Our linguistic ancestors. If not for the society they built and the language they cultivated, the way we speak, read, and spell today would be inestimably different. How many great-grandparents of English were there? Five thousand? Twenty-five thousand? We'll never know. But their numbers were surely less than those crowding a modern-day football stadium. Estimates of Britain's *total* population in the fifth century suggest around five hundred thousand people.[7]

Through the ferry's rain-streaked windows, I finally spotted the White Cliffs of Dover, looking like the face of a chalk-colored glacier. Imagine this voyage from the perspective of sixth-century migrants. They would've heard bits of information about Britain, but they had no way to distinguish fact from fiction. As the coastline came into focus, this new land must have looked simultaneously beautiful and foreboding.*

During the early period of Old English, four major dialects emerged, representing the four major kingdoms of the land. But one of them began to outpace the others in terms of geographic breadth and influence. The Old English dialect of Wessex became the written standard, as much as it was possible to have a standard language in a time of clashing kingdoms and no mass communication other than books copied by hand. Because it was the nerve center of Old English writing, Wessex was the first stop on my spelling tour.

WHEN I PROPOSED an orthography-themed road trip through England, linguist David Crystal's reply was: "cool idea." One of the planet's preeminent scholars of English, Crystal has been described as a British national treasure. He has written dozens of books, some on language and many on English specifically, and he's the go-to source for matters of language as varied as punctuation in a sixteenth-century text, the influence of Northumbrian dialect on Old English, Shakespearean rhyme, the tragedy of dying languages, and the linguistic significance of text messaging.

I caught up with Crystal and his wife, Hilary, near Brighton, in the southern England county of Sussex. To my relief, David was not nearly as stern as his author photograph suggests. He still has the professorial air, but it's softened by a look that makes me think of a jovial werewolf. The gray hair atop his large head is thin, but it's

---

*Not all the invaders would have taken this northwesterly route. Some arrived in the south, others to the east.

long and wavy, joining up with a much thicker mane toward his ears and neck. His sideburns flow seamlessly into a white beard that's full enough to warrant its own gloved search by airport security personnel. His large, arcing nose supports owlish glasses that magnify piercing brown eyes. The effect would produce an intimidating gaze, were it not for the adjacent laugh lines and frequent accentuation of them.

David was a few hours away from delivering the keynote address at the Society for Editors and Proofreaders's annual conference. Editors and freelance proofreaders are a solitary lot, but get a bunch of them together and look out. First we were treated to a round of remix poetry, in which works by William Carlos Williams and Dylan Thomas were tweaked to create a plethora of puns about grammar headaches, rambling emails from hassling authors, and stingy publishers. Then we sang along to the Twelve Days of the Schedule (pronounced "shejule" in Britain). The finale round goes like this:

On the twelfth day of the schedule
My client sent to me:
Twelve sheets of briefing
Eleven text equations
Ten symbols lurking
Nine sexist pronouns
Eight footnotes missing
Seven misquotations
Six clauses dangling
Five chapters more!
Four fuzzy graphs
Three locked files

Two authors French
And a typescript all neat and tidee[8]

It was 10:00 p.m. before he gave his talk to the starstruck audience, but Crystal was on his game. His speech moved seamlessly from the place that holds the title of longest name on earth (Taumatawhakatangihangakoauauotamateaturipukakapikimaungahoronukupokaiwhenuakitanatahu, New Zealand), to the study of words with no repeated letters, to a discussion of word pairings, known to linguists as collective nouns, such as: "a gaggle of geese," "a tiding of ravens," "a body of pathologists," and "a rash of dermatologists."

The next morning the Crystals and I hit the road. Hilary deftly steered the beige sedan through serpentine country lanes as we made our way to focal points in the story—or stories, as David would say—of English spelling. Surprisingly, to this American anyway, the first major act in the story of English orthography isn't set in London. As the epicenter of British economy and culture, not to mention central command for what was once the world's most powerful empire, it would follow that London is the linguistic incubator from which English was born. In many ways that's true: Crucial events and people in the evolution of our language were indeed based there. But not during the Old English period, which runs roughly from the sixth through the eleventh century. "King Alfred's Wessex was the place to be," said Crystal. "That's why I first want to take you to Winchester," the town in the heart of Wessex from where Alfred built a kingdom and fortified a language.

In the southern portion of the country, the Old English dialect of Wessex was taking off, in large part because the local literature was so closely connected to the Church. It was the monks in scriptoriums, or writing rooms, who did all the writing—sermons, poems, and official documents. They took the spoken dialects of the land and gave them life on the page. As they carried out this task, they wrote phonetically, trying to match sounds of words with letters to represent them.[9] With varieties of Old English spread about the countryside, different monks making their own decisions about sound-to-letter correspondence, as well as inevitable copying errors, variation in Old English spelling was unavoidable.[10] Still, sound was the principal guide for spelling, which meant the orthography of the Wessex dialect, or West Saxon, was largely phonetic. The standard was: Try to write like it sounds.[11]

Monks throughout ancient Britain were busily scribing away, but the ones who most influenced the language were based at Winchester, working for King Alfred and his successors. Beginning in the year 871, Alfred became king of Wessex. In the decades leading up to his reign, the Danes had forcibly acquired much of the northern and interior portions of the island, steadily expanding southward and threatening wholesale takeover. Alfred pushed them back, thus earning the moniker, "Alfred the Great."

Had Alfred failed against the Danes, English may never have existed. When thinking about the history of English, the impact of such "what ifs" gets diluted by the sheer frequency of occasions when the language was in jeopardy. On the other hand, the myth of language purity can be so intractable that revisiting times when English was almost obliterated reminds us that language is not a holy doctrine. It's more like an organism, evolving through a gradual process of accumulated accidents and narrow escapes. The same might be said of our sometimes torturous spelling system. Nudge history a little to the left or right, and English orthography may have taken a totally different path.

Alfred's abilities as a political and military leader were matched by his vision for education, which over the long run helped cata-pult English into the future. He recognized the power not just of knowledge but also of knowledge taught and learned in one's native tongue. Lamenting the loss of linguistic heritage at the hands of the invading and book-destroying Vikings, he wrote of his desire to translate important books "into the language that we can all under-stand," and of his commitment to teach "young people who are now freemen in England . . . how to read written English well."

While Latin was the language of the Church, Old English had persisted as the language of the people. But how to write it down? Some Old English sounds had no corresponding letter in Latin, which meant the monks had to improvise, borrowing the occasional letter from the local alphabets, and mixing them into the Roman alphabet, the one we use now, give or take a couple of letters.[12] Like the spoken language of the day, the Old English writing system was in a state of flux.

Alfred pushed for a language revival. He ordered the monks serv-ing him at Winchester's Hyde Abbey to translate the Bible, sermons, and legal texts from Latin into the West Saxon dialect. It wasn't a purely altruistic policy. Bolstering religious education was an effec-tive way, as Crystal writes, "to win God's support for victory over the pagan Danes and to consolidate loyalty to himself [Alfred] as a Christian king." It worked, as far as anyone can tell, and most of the surviving Old English texts are written in the West Saxon dialect, in which we find many familiar words, such as *feoll* (fell), *god* (good), *heard* (hard), and *swurd* (sword).[13] Alfred's prestige and the thriv-ing monastery at Winchester enabled the monks of Hyde Abbey to travel the country, visiting other monasteries to share sermons and news from around the region. In so doing, they spread their pre-ferred dialect and spellings in an almost viruslike fashion.

Nowadays, the most visitable part of the Hyde Abbey ruins are wedged between a city park and a neighborhood of redbrick row houses along King Alfred Place. Remnants of stone walls and other structures are found alongside a stream that runs through the town. The Crystals and I walked to the barn-sized stone building at the center of the scattered ruins. On the outside, the split rocks in the flint-cobble walls glistened in the sunshine. Inside the bare single room, the air was cool and a slight breeze gently shook strands of dust-coated cobwebs.

Inspecting the aged stone walls, Crystal nodded. "We're standing inside the cloister where a more standardized English was almost going to be." The English of Alfred the Great and his followers was on the road to stardom. The Abbey with the most influence in the political sense in turn had the most influence on orthography because there were no dictionaries, grammar guides, language pundits or spelling books to consult as lexicographical authorities. Were we to somehow cancel out the major historical and linguistic events on the near horizon of the first millennium, we would have today a language significantly easier to write. Back then, most spellings represented—not perfectly but closely—the way a word sounded when read aloud.

Keep in mind, though, that even this far back in the history of English the name of the game is melting pot. The West Saxon dialect was mixing with dialects from farther north, as well as incorporating Danish and Old French words. The stewlike nature of the language would intensify in the centuries to come; think of a bungalow-dwelling sushi, avocado, and opossum connoisseur (or any group of words with origins in India, England, Japan, Mexico, Virginia, and France). But admixing was already well under way in Wessex.

Although the Old English of Alfred's time was mostly phonetic and standardized, there's no evidence that a notion of misspelling existed. Who was to say what was correct, and by what authority? The dialect of West Saxon thrived because Alfred's kingdom thrived. His power meant his preferred language—and the prolific writing produced by monks at Hyde and other abbeys around Winchester—traveled far and wide. Then again, in the minds of the people, many of whom were illiterate anyway, the particulars of this emerging orthography went unnoticed. A notion of more formal Standard English was still centuries away.

Yet there were clues that an ethic of correctness in writing was taking shape, one that would influence future ideas about propriety generally and proper spelling specifically. One of the most important surviving texts of the Old English period, known as the *Colloquy* and written by an abbot named Ælfric (pronounced "al-fritch") around the year 1000, shows an intense concern for scribal accuracy, but in reference to content and words, not spelling per se. The *Colloquy* imagines a role-playing exercise in which students pose questions to their teacher, and the teacher thunders back with instruction. It sounds like "great fun," said Crystal, something along the lines of: Q: "Oh teacher, what shall we do?" A: "Study your grammar." Q: "And if we don't?" A: "I shall beat you." In one section, Ælfric writes:

> *He does great evil who writes carelessly, unless he correct it.*
> *It is as though he turn true doctrine into false error.*
> *Therefore everyone should make straight that which he before*
> *   bent crooked, if he will be guiltless at God's doom.*[14]

Even though I have a rocky relationship with spelling, now is as good a time as any to mention that I'm not an orthography anarchist. Standards matter; how are we going to understand one another without a commonly understood code of written communication? Likewise, correctness matters. Correct spelling in the sense of adhering to commonly agreed upon conventions makes for efficient exchange of written information and ideas. But there's nuance here.

Consider the unit of length known as the meter. Once defined as the length of a rod equal to 1/10,000,000 the distance between the equator and the poles, the modern definition is 1/299,792,458 the distance light travels in one second. Such gorgeous specificity! The meter was first developed in France and the International Prototype Metre bar is located in the International Bureau of Weights and Measures in Paris. The razor-sharp definition and jargony institutional backing provide a standard accepted by everyone.

For English words, we have nothing of the sort. Yet Ælfric's linking of carelessness in writing with "great evil" foreshadows two ideas that thread through much of the story of English spelling. The first is the perceived relationship between accuracy in writing and what it means to be a virtuous human being. The second is the distinction between standard and correct English. "Standard English" is the language that hovers around the most widely accepted norms. "Correct English" is language, spoken or written, deemed acceptable by select people.

In Alfred's Wessex, the standard for English was one of orthographic liberalism, guided by scribes' good-faith efforts to make their words intelligible by matching spelling to sound. In Winchester, I could see more clearly the Old English roots of today's words, and the road down which English was heading at the end of the last millennium. But I also saw that I had a long way to go before reaching modern spelling and our attitudes about it. Ælfric was a stickler for accurate content but not spelling, and outside the scriptorium and elite circles close to the king, people probably didn't notice or care about orthography. Can you imagine it: A society in which attitudes toward spelling were more Haight-Ashbury than harsh judgment? No grade-school humiliation courtesy of the remedial spelling books. No more chiding my sister, who once spelled the word *opportunity* with one *p* in the first sentence of a college application. No damn bees.

As we left the ruins of Hyde Abbey, Crystal, aware of my spelling woes, offered this sobering synopsis: "You were born about one thousand years too late." Had the linguistic push by King Alfred and the monks of Hyde Abbey continued unabated, it's reasonable to imagine that the 1.4 billion people who speak, read, and write English today would be speaking, reading, and writing in the Old English dialect of Alfred's West Saxon, or some derivative of it, with a less troublesome spelling system to boot.

But that's not how it happened. The French came.

THREE

REGIME CHANGE

Christ and his apostles taught the people in that tongue that was
most known to the people. Why should not men do now so?

John Wycliffe

M Y TRAIN SLOWED THROUGH the Bo Peep Tunnel before stopping at the tiny station in the southern England hamlet of
Battle. I followed signs up the hill toward the village center, past the
Chequers Inn Restaurant and Ye Olde Café. Looming straight ahead
were the walls of Battle Abbey. Soon after the epic Battle of Hastings
in 1066, William the Conqueror ordered the construction of this
abbey to honor the dead—penance for all that killing.

A trail loops around the famous battlefield, alongside patches of
thistle, ever-encroaching blackberries, and a few oak and birch trees.
My handheld audio guide played a soundtrack of clashing metal and
groans of injured men, and described the wartime scene down to the
personalities, strategies, and armaments of the day, "clubs, scythes,
slings, and spears." On this bucolic hillside almost one thousand years
ago, William the Conqueror won the kingdom of England. In one
day, an army of less than ten thousand men gained for their leader

a territorial prize inhabited by some 1.5 million people, beginning a centuries-long period of French rule that would change English culture and language forever.* The fight was by no means a blowout. At first, the English held their ground with an advantageous hilltop position. Locking arms and shields, they were relatively unaffected by the enemy arrows and charging cavalry. Things were looking up for King Harold, the Englishmen, and the more standardized orthography of Old English. Harold must have felt a rush of confidence. Just weeks earlier, Vikings had attacked in the north, and Harold and his army had defeated them soundly.

But there was no time for celebration. Harold received word that the Normans had crossed the Channel and were sacking villages in the southeast. In less than two weeks, he marched his men some 250 miles from Yorkshire south to this spot on Senlac Hill, stopping only briefly in London before pressing ahead.

In contrast to Harold's men, who must've been exhausted, William's men were fresh and well armed. They also had a supernatural edge. Before launching the invasion, William received the Pope's blessing for his campaign; God was apparently on his side. To the Normans, takeover of Britain was not an invasion, but a reclaiming of God-given property. William had at one time been promised the throne of England.

Inspired by papal approval and their powerful leader, the Normans repeatedly attacked the English shield wall despite minimal results. William needed a new tactic, so he instructed his cavalry to

---

*I'm casually interchanging "French" with "Norman." The muddier truth of the matter is that there was Old Norman, Old French, and Anglo-Norman, not to mention other regional dialects, let alone the fact that the Normans were themselves of Scandinavian descent.

perform a fake retreat. Just as the English defenses relaxed, the Normans pounced from the side and broke through the wall. Gradually, the Normans pushed their way up the hill and by evening the battle was over. The French, with their language, had begun their takeover.

Some historians speculate that Harold was overconfident after beating back the Vikings. A fierce patriot, Harold may have allowed fury to trump prudence, rushing to engage the Normans when he should have taken a little more time to let his troops recuperate. Rebuilding a few pillaged villages is a lot easier than winning back a kingdom, and a couple of days of rest may have boosted his army's chance for success. Whether a London layover would have altered the battle outcome is anyone's guess. But the fact that Harold's armor still carried the dried blood of the Vikings adds to the recurring impression that the fate of the English language had been swayed by forces as minute as one man's decision on one afternoon nearly one thousand years ago.

When people talk about wars, a common refrain is that if it weren't for the heroes who sacrificed so much, we'd all be speaking (language X) now. Following the Norman invasion, French usurped an estimated 85 percent of the Old English vocabulary. Old English words like *wisen* (attire), *munuccliff* (abbey), *milce* (grace), and so many others were fossilized. For a while there, it looked like we were all going to be speaking French.[1] Why didn't that happen?

William and his successors owned England and subjugated the English people, but they didn't go out of their way to eliminate the local tongue. In the centuries following the Norman invasion, England was essentially trilingual, with other dialects sprinkled around the countryside. French was the language of government, law, military, and all things upper crust. Latin was the language of the Church. And English was the language of the farm, street, and tavern. Through the period known as Middle English, which begins with the Battle of Hastings and ends around 1500, the language slowly shifted from Old English to a chic newer version, infused with words of French derivation.

By some estimates ten thousand words were introduced into English from French, perhaps thousands more. This lexical deluge can be seen right on the battlefield. Words like *soldier* (from *soudier*), *court* (from *curt*), *peasant* (from *paisant*), and *guard* (from *garde*).* There's *traitor* (*traitre*), *govern* (*governer*), *authority* (*authorité*), *prison* (*prisun*), and *chancellor* (*canceler*). The incoming vocabulary mirrored the spheres of French dominance. Law, military, courts, cuisine, fashion, social classes—these were the sectors of society into which the word infusion was most pervasive. Over time, the speakers of English took the new words and made them their own. *Arrest* (*arrêter*) and *judge* (*juge*); *throne* (*trone*) and *nobility* (*nobilité*); *lemons* (*limons*) and *grapes* (*grappes*).[2]

If the French weren't to blame for enough orthographic turmoil already, we can also thank them for "the very notion of spelling." Linguist Seth Lerer writes:

> [It] comes not from Old English but Old French—for the word *spellian* in Old English meant to talk or tell a story or to move with speech (it is the root of the Old English word *god-spell*, the good talk, and thus our Modern English "gospel"). The Old French word *espelir*, by contrast, meant to set out by letters, and it is only late in

---

*Linguist Vivian Cook points out that "French spoken in England after the Norman Conquest (1066) came from Normandy rather than Paris. Hence English often has pairs of words from both sources, for example the Anglo-Norman 'w' versus the Parisian 'g.'" Consider: ward/guard, warden/guardian, and wile/guile. (Vivian Cook, *Accomodating Brocolli in the Cemetary: Or Why Can't Anybody Spell?* p.6)

Middle English that this word converges with *spellian* to produce a verb, *spellen*, that could mean both speak and spell . . . [as in] "to form by letters."[3]

The arrival of French institutions, vocabulary, and culture both subverted and enriched the English language, while adding a layer of confusion onto spelling that would only worsen over time.

But by the Middle Ages, English was slowly reasserting itself. English women married into the homes of French barons and aristocrats, and brought their first language with them. Many of their children would have been bilingual, giving English a foothold on a higher rung of the social ladder. The Black Death dealt another blow to French and Latin. In 1350, an estimated one-third of the population of England was wiped out by the disease. Especially hard-hit were densely settled areas and the monastic communities of the clergy. Many of the survivors were people on the periphery—the dregs of society, as one writer put it—and their primary language was English. By 1381, thirteen-year-old King Richard II was conducting affairs of state in English, and the language could sometimes be heard in the hallowed halls of Oxford.[4]

As the language started making its way back into the mainstream, once again scribes played a crucial role as agents of spelling change. During the centuries of French rule, the people in power kept detailed government records, all written in French. English began creeping back into fashion in the 1300s, but scribes, especially those working in the courts, were still very much under the influence of French linguistic traditions. As a result, they sometimes superimposed their preferred, French-style spellings over the English ones, as in the case of *cwen* becoming *queen*, *cwic* becoming *quick*, *cwellan* becoming *quell*, and *scip* becoming *ship*.[5]

A picture of worrisome variation begins to emerge: the *e* instead of the *i* in *lemon*; the *ai* in *paisant* became *ea* in *peasant*; the appearance of *d* in *judge* (to say nothing of *edge*, *sledge*, *wedge*, and *ledge*). Why? Because spelling is created by people giving written form to words in ways that are familiar to them at that time. Scribes during the Middle English period weren't lexicographers or linguists with an eye on big-picture orthographic consistency. English spelling was the result of monks and scribes essentially winging it. In Alfred's Wessex, words were based on phonetic interpretations of Old English. When the scribes of Norman-occupied England set to spelling out words, they had to reconcile the now-quite-French nature of the lexicon.

Another major factor affecting English's comeback was a best-seller called *The Canterbury Tales*. Geoffrey Chaucer wrote much more than that one book, but his tales within the tale of a London-to-Canterbury pilgrimage had an impact on the shape of English unlike any other book in history, with the possible exception of the Bible. By the time Chaucer comes on the scene in the late 1300s, English was no longer viewed as the dirty language of the poor, yet literary types still felt it lacked the grace and expressiveness of French or Italian.

Chaucer saw and heard it differently. He delighted in and de-voured the sounds of English spoken on the streets of London. For Chaucer, the language was still raw, malleable. French was on the decline but not kaput, and English still had a great deal of regional variation. Within this linguistic chaos, Chaucer heard something magnificent: a language with the potential to be as colorful, en-chanting, expansive, and precise as any the world had ever seen, if not more so because of its penchant for seizing foreign words and enlisting them in its ranks.

Chaucer didn't set out to prove English's worth or establish new spellings. Aside from people like David Crystal, most writers don't write with linguistic evolution in mind; they simply communicate in the way most natural to them. Chaucer was no different. But his genius, or an aspect of his genius, was in capitalizing on the flexibility and breadth of the language of his time in a way no one ever had, resulting in a lexicographic rainstorm of ingenuity. He was putting the English of the people to paper, while spicing it up with French. The opening lines to *The Canterbury Tales* contain a handful of French borrowings:

> *Whán that Apríllé with hise shourés soote*
> *The droghte of March hath percéd to the roote,*
> *And bathéd every veyne in swich licóur*
> *Of which vertú engendred is the flour . . .*

> *When April with its sweet showers*
> *has pierced the drought of March to the root,*
> *and bathed every vein in such liquid*
> *from which strength the flower is engendered . . .*

The same goes for the beginning of his geeky *Treatise on the Astrolabe*, written for his son as instruction for using that scientific instrument. Reading it aloud brings to mind a Steve Martin spoof of a French accent, and drives home the transitional nature of the language of Chaucer's time: "I apercyve wel by certeyne evidences thyn abilite to lerne sciences touching nombres and proporciouns; and as wel considre I thy besy praier in special to lerne the tretys of the Astrelabie." ("I can well see from several signs your ability to learn about the sciences to do with numbers and proportions; and I also take note of your earnest request especially to acquire knowledge about the treatise on the astrolabe.")[6] Chaucer could be blamed for certain spellings today, although not many. Huge lexicographic changes were yet to come, and spelling was still all over the map; one review of a dozen *Canterbury Tales* manuscripts, for instance, includes multiple spellings of the words *work* (*werche, worke, werke,* etc.) and *though* (*thogh, thouh,* etc.). They all worked, though. Many times the same manuscript included variable spellings for the same word.[7] Nevertheless, as a singularly influential writer, Chaucer affected the linguistic sensibilities of orthography decision makers to come: scribes, other writers, copyists and, soon, printers.

At about the same time that Chaucer was quilling the *Canterbury Tales*, another "standardizing force," as Crystal put it, was being written in a church parish about one hundred miles north of London. To examine this facet of the Middle English period and its influence on today's Standard English, David, Hilary, and I traveled to St. Mary's Church in the town of Lutterworth.

Entering the building, David rubbed his forehead, as if trying to slow the torrent of words, derivations, dialects, texts, and historical events rushing through his brain. "You have to ask: Why did so much of the East Midlands dialect become the standard for what then became Standard English?" he said. The Old English that developed farther south during the reign of Alfred had been crushed by the Norman invasion. As new versions of English sprouted throughout the countryside, what lifted one above the others?

Chaucer is only part of the answer. The expanding sheep-wool industry catalyzed a great deal of trade, both economic and linguistic, between the middle part of the country, London, and eastern port towns. "So as they went east and south, the people of the Midlands brought with them their way of talking and writing," Crystal explained. Meanwhile, the academic enclaves of Oxford and

Cambridge, also in this middle-ish part of the country, were focal points of linguistic growth and cross-pollination with words from French, Latin, and other languages. French still held sway, but English, no longer viewed as the vulgar third-rate tongue, was beginning to infiltrate the classroom.

And with a bang it infiltrated the Church. To successfully bring God to the everyman, a fourteenth-century preacher named John Wycliffe felt the Bible should be translated from Latin into English. From an ornately sculpted pulpit in St. Mary's of Lutterworth, he dared to suggest that the Pope's word (*No English in my church!*) might not be identical to God's word (*Love thy neighbor*).* The Crystals led me toward a glass case near the church entrance. "This is it," said David, tapping the glass. Below were two thick, ever-so-fragile-looking books opened to a middle page revealing colorful drawings and lines of handwritten text. The label next to them read: "Two volumes which comprise the first translation of the entire Bible into the English Language, completed about AD 1380 by John de Wycliffe, while Rector of this Parish." The translations are, in the words of the church, "blessings which God bestowed on the English people by this earliest version of the holy scriptures in their mother tongue."

The idea of translated Bibles was unpopular with the Church's top brass, as democratizing religious reforms tend to be. Yet Wycliffe charged ahead. He was later condemned, but the linguistic impact of this first English Bible was irreversible, and rapid dissemination of copies helped catapult what is known as the East Midlands dialect of Middle English into pole position as standard language of the land and of the future.

---

*Despite the death of so many clergy due to the plague, Latin had held on as the language of God and the Bible.

The Church was able to reassert the superiority of Latin for a little while, but soon other translators picked up where Wycliffe left off, most famous among them William Tyndale. In the sixteenth century, Tyndale was smuggling English editions of the Bible into England from Antwerp, until he was ambushed by authorities and burned at the stake for heresy and treason. His last words were: "Lord, open the King of England's Eyes!" But again, the influence outlasted the man. Roughly 80 percent of the wording in the first King James Bible (1611) is the same as that used in Tyndale's edition.[8]

Wycliffe's Bible gave an essential boost to the East Midlands dialect, and may have even influenced some of Chaucer's work and words.[9] The vocabulary of the Bible isn't as impressive as that of *The Canterbury Tales*, although some words do make their debut in Wycliffe's translation: *communication, injury, envy, novelty, birthday, madness*.[10] Then again, like Chaucer, Wycliffe had limited direct impact on spelling; tectonic orthographic shifts loomed just around the corner, and both men were still writing at a time of considerable spelling variation. Wycliffe's Bible was rife with variable spellings like *counseil/councel, stod/stood, chayer/chaier, shal/schal* (for *shall*).[11] The key here, though, is that Wycliffe and Chaucer are essential players in the wider story of English spelling because there's no such thing as a spelling standard without a more standardized language. That standardization gets under way during the period of Middle English, and two of the most significant forces shaping Middle English were John Wycliffe and Geoffrey Chaucer.

A third force that helps cement Middle English and accelerate the development of more standard spellings is the Chancery court at Westminster. This was the civil service office handling many of the legal affairs of the kingdom. Through drafting, copying, and dispatching formal orders and writs from the king's court, these scribes spread words across the country in written forms that they, and really their bosses, saw fit. They had a keen interest in consistent orthography: it improved comprehensibility with audiences speaking various English dialects, and also imbued documents with legal and formal authority.[12]

They certainly had their hands full. Before the late Middle English period, *receive*, for example, can be found as *receve*, *rassaif*, *recyve*, *receyf*, and in no less than forty other iterations. *People* can be found as *peple*, *peopel*, *pepulle*, and many other forms, just as *church* took the shape of *cirche*, *kirc*, *chyrche*, and *chrch*, among others.[13] Crystal points out the dearth of scholarship into the precise influence of the Chancery scribes on English and its spelling code, but it's clear that a number of spellings were settled by this crew of government administrators. The word *shall*, formerly *schal* or even *xal*, was given its modern form by the Chancery wordsmiths, just as *bot* became *but*, *thise* became *these*, and *seide* became *saide*.[14] Convention was emerging, but that didn't mean the scribes were shy about deliberately using some older and decidedly nonphonetic spellings—*high*, *though*, *nought*, *slaughter*, while also, and probably inadvertently, continuing to use a number of variable spellings, such as *lowely/loweli*, *any/eny/ony*, and *which/wich*.[15]

AS THE CRYSTALS and I wandered around St. Mary's inspecting fading frescos and discussing the Catholic Church's backlash against English after Wycliffe's gutsy translation, we came to a peculiar architectural detail, the squint. A rectangular hole in the wall alongside the main area for seating, behind which lies an additional row of pews, the squint's purpose is unknown. One hypothesis is that while Mass was under way in the sanctuary, another service might have been held in this smaller side chapel. Through the squint, people could keep an eye on what was happening in first class. Another possibility is that this auxiliary area was for lepers and other village outcasts. Outsiders were permitted to watch the service, but only from a safe and segregated distance.

Sometime after poking my head through the squint, I realized that my journey with the Crystals was having a reforming influence on me and my thinking about what it means to be a poor speller. What was coming into focus was not only the gap between language and spelling, but also the chance-ridden history of English orthography. People communicate ideas through language, whereas spelling, as Chaucer, Wycliffe, and the Chancery scribes must have known, is only the tool for encoding the language, and an imperfect and shifting one at that. Spelling decisions weren't random, but they were human, carrying all the folly, inconsistency, bias, and creativity that goes with that territory.

That English is such a mutt of a language only served to make the resulting spellings that much harder. Old English had already been borrowing from, and interbreeding with, Dutch and Latin before the Norman invasion. The arrival of Norman French opened the floodgates for more linguistic mixing and orthographic variability. After a few centuries of French rule and language, Middle English received a huge boost from Chaucer, Wycliffe, and the Chancery style.

Yet as widely disseminated and lasting an impact as their writings had, their words still only reached audiences by way of handwritten manuscripts. But not for long.

FOUR

PAGE SETUP

"Loo, what sholde a man in thyse dayes now wryte, egges or eyren."

from William Caxton's 1490 Prologue to his translation of Virgil's Aeneid

THE RECTANGULAR IRON CASE holding the words looked heavy in the man's outstretched hand, like a gold bar. He used two round dog-skin leather tools with wooden handles to apply the ink. I was sitting in the demonstration room at the Gutenberg Museum in Mainz, Germany, along with a dozen schoolchildren wearing Puma and Vans sneakers, blue jeans and sweatshirts. We were watching a museum staffer operate a replica of a fifteenth-century printing press.

One of the bigger students, thirteen or fourteen years old, volunteered to pull on the thick, two-foot-long lever that pushes the paper down onto the raised rows of inky type. The boy put his foot up on the side of the press for leverage, then leaned back and pulled with all his might. The staffer displayed the freshly printed page and the boy's classmates applauded politely.

No one ever applauded for Johannes Gutenberg until late in his life. His invention sparked sweeping changes to civilization as we know it: government, science, religion, language and, yes, spelling. Ideas—explosive ideas about, say, religious reformation or democracy—had a mobility they never could have had in the centuries of scriptorium-produced books. The Internet is quite something, but so far it can't add anything like "spawned the Enlightenment" to its résumé.[1]

Gutenberg was from a well-to-do fifteenth-century family that had inherited a bunch of real estate. Yet his father was looked down upon by the neighbors in Mainz for not working for a living, and, perhaps more so, because he mismanaged his assets and struggled to stay in the black. Preparing for the possibility that he might have to work, young Johannes decided that learning a trade skill was in his best interest. He worked as a goldsmith at the mint, where he mastered the art of metallurgy.[2] Over the course of more than a decade, Gutenberg melted countless batches of metal, pouring it into molds where, after partially cooling, the unfinished coins would be ready for engraving. During those years at the mint, Gutenberg must have sketched in his mind his futuristic device.

Someone else would have come up with it, eventually. By the fifteenth century, the public appetite for books was pushing the copying capacity of scribes to the limit. Stories about faraway lands (Marco Polo's exploration of Asia); interest in current events (the Black Death); and an ever-expanding market for the Bible all added to a widespread hunger for knowledge. The Renaissance was coming, but there was no way to mass-produce books and share new information, until suddenly there was: Within forty-five years of the invention of the printing press in the late 1440s, some ten million books would be printed.[3]

Gutenberg was famously secretive about the device he spent twenty years perfecting, nervous that someone might steal his idea.[4]

He had no patent laws to protect his intellectual property and his invention was uncomplicated enough that it easily could have been copied. But when it came time to open a business, Gutenberg didn't have the capital to proceed. He sought out loans, first from his brother-in-law and then from a local lender. Fiscal mismanagement was in his genes, though, and as the costs for his early printing efforts mounted, Gutenberg couldn't keep up.

In the end, Gutenberg's downfall had nothing to do with knock-offs. Just as he was finally printing and selling some books, his business partner lost patience and took him to court. The famous inventor's debt led to a lost lawsuit and the forfeiture of his printing press, workshop equipment, and a bulk of whatever money he'd earned from sales. Late in life, he was recognized for his achievement by the Archbishop of Mainz, and even received a small award. But the goldsmith who made coins for a living before inventing one of the most important devices of the millennium spent much of his life battling debt.

Yet history has been kind to the father of the printing press. Nobody really remembers Johann Fust, the business partner who sued Gutenberg. We remember and honor the inventor and the impact his "Werk der Bucher" (*work of the books*) had on humanity in the 550 years since.* The Chinese had come up with a method for printing one thousand years prior, but the brilliance of Gutenberg's creation was the moveable metal type that allowed typesetters to disassemble text letter by letter after printing, for reuse in the next composition. The use of metal was also a breakthrough. Previous printing technology used wood blocks for type, which warp over time.

---

*The expression comes from court records from the Fust lawsuit.

Before the advent of printing, spelling was erratic. How could it not have been? Monks in scriptoriums scattered throughout the countryside and working in near isolation were hired to copy texts for individuals or institutions. There were no set spelling rules and no notions of correctly written English. On the contrary, the monks likely tried to write in a way that would best cater to the dialect and familiar spellings of a particular client. The point was to make *that* book readable, not to invent a spelling system for all books.

Chancery scribes introduced some conventions, but it was printing that led to a settled orthography. Mass production meant that printers began the gradual process of deciding on a single spelling for a word, or maybe a few variants, and weeding out the rest. This was still well before anything we would identify today as a house style, which is publishing-industry speak for "the way we do things," with *things* being spelling, punctuation, and grammar. Spellings in printing houses of the late fifteenth and sixteenth centuries were a function of each printer's interest in economical completion of the task. How does one spell a word? Just like you did the last three times. The process of settling spelling wasn't sudden, but Gutenberg's invention marked the beginning of the end for unbridled English orthography.

The demonstration at the Gutenberg Museum was a helpful primer and gave me a chance to pay homage to the man and his invention. But the museum staffer skipped over the essential step, so far as spelling is concerned: letter selection. I wanted to know what life and work were like for the men operating the early presses, constructing the words and composing the text of the first printed books. In Europe's earliest printing houses, those men held our orthographic fate in their hands.

* * *

A FEW TRAIN connections later and I stood in a cobbled square outside the Plantin-Moretus Museum in Antwerp. The founder of Plantin Press, Christoffel Plantin, had come to Antwerp from Paris sometime around 1549 with designs on learning the trade of bookbinding. Soon after his arrival he was attacked in what was apparently a case of mistaken identity, and one of his arms was permanently damaged. Plantin no longer had the dexterity required for bookbinding, but he could pull the lever of a printing press. So he started a publishing business, first called Du Gulden Passer (The Golden Compasses), and later Plantin Press. For the next three hundred years, it was one of the most successful and esteemed printing houses in Europe. The stone and brick building facing Vrijdagmarkt Square was both the family home and the production workshop. Today it houses the two oldest printing presses in the world and a priceless collection of antiques, tapestries, paintings, and of course, books.

Guido Latre walked briskly to greet me. He's a short man with round eyeglasses and a mostly bald head. Latre grew up in Flanders, where he earned money to pay for his first visit to England by digging up World War I copper fuses on his family's farm and selling them as souvenirs to British visitors to a nearby war cemetery. "I couldn't speak English, but I memorized the sentence: 'Want a souvenir, sir? It's one hundred Belgian francs.'"[5] Today, Latre is Professor of English literature and culture at the University of Louvain-la-Neuve, and he knows the Plantin-Moretus Museum inside and out.

We started in the production area, a ground-floor room lined with presses along the wall. Opposite them were cases full of "type," small metal blocks (called bars) with one side bearing a letter molded in relief. The setting felt like a factory without machines. "We're still centuries from the industrial revolution," said Latre. "Yet this was really industrial-scale production." In the time it would have taken a monk to make a single copy of the Bible or *The Canterbury Tales*, the seventy or eighty employees at Plantin, printing four, sometimes even six, pages a minute and on multiple presses, could produce a few thousand copies. Books went from being expensive treasures to something an everyday person could buy with a week's wages. Ideas, and the words encoding them, were reaching more people than ever.

The atmosphere inside workshops like that of Plantin Press had a direct influence on modern-day spelling. "Try to imagine the pressure in this room," said Latre. While one man worked the press, another man, the "compositor," stood by the case full of letters and rapidly composed rows of text. The cases are long rectangular trays with dozens of divided sections, each filled with small metal letter blocks.

Every case was organized based on the frequency of a letter's use. The larger, capitalized letters were used less often, and therefore stored in the upper section of the tray, and vice-versa for the non-capitalized, or lowercase, letters. This sectioned layout was an internationally recognized standard, and although typesetting is now an obsolete craft, the language of the trade is still with us; it's where we get the terms uppercase and lowercase, and a family of one size and style of type was known as a font.

The compositor's job was to pick out the type and set it into the chases, those rectangular trays holding the lines of text. He was laying out the words letter by letter, most likely copying from a manuscript (written in whatever language) set in front of him. He would have encountered countless inconsistencies of spelling, in different manuscripts or even in the same manuscript, but there was no rule or system in place for addressing matters of spelling. On the contrary, shop employees were paid by the page, which meant the men running the presses would have had little time for slow compositors deliberating over their compositions. "Remember," said Latre, "a good printer is pressing multiple pages a minute." When it came to spelling, "they could not afford to have the patience of a monk in a scriptorium. Publishing was no longer a cottage industry," which meant "no one bothered with the niceties of local dialects," and there was little consideration for orthographic consistency or lack thereof.

As if working fast didn't make the job stressful enough, there were other challenges too. The type was tiny, some letter bars were small enough to fit comfortably inside a thimble. The typesetters also had to create a mirror image of the text, from right to left, so that the press would transpose normal text onto the page. In addition, compositors and printers needed to neatly align their margins. From the sixteenth century through to the present, printed pages were seen as more elegant and formal if the left and right margins were straight and uniform, as you can tell from the book you're now holding. Printers trained compositors to carefully fill out their lines, fiddling with words to get them to fit. Adding or axing a final -e on the end of a word was an effective way to even out margins, with apparently little or no cost to legibility or aesthetic.[6]

Many printers of the earliest English-language texts were not native English speakers, and some of them may have known very little English at all. Look once again to the first lines of *The Canterbury Tales*, "When April with its sweet showers":

Whán that Apríllé with hise shourés soote
The droghte of March hath percéd to the roote,
And bathéd every veyne in swich licóur
Of which vertú engendred is the flour . . .

In some texts, *April* was written "Aprille," and *his* represented as "hise," even if, as Crystal explains, "[t]he metre suggests that there is no *-e* pronounced in *Aprille* and *hise*, but that there is one in *shoures*—'shoor-uhs'. But people disagree over whether *soote* was 'soht' or 'soht-uh' [meaning *sweet*]. A foreign compositor would get the impression that final *-e* was random, and that he could put it in or leave it out as he wished."[7] Translation: Spellings that were close enough were good enough.

Employees at Plantin and elsewhere in the sixteenth century also probably gave us the *h* in words like *ghost* and *ghastly*. The Dutch spelling convention for a comparable sound was written as *gh*, so the typesetters superimposed their spelling preferences onto the words they were constructing, just as scribes of Norman-occupied England had done.[8] For a while, *girl* (*gherle*) and *goose* (*ghoos*) were *h*-ified as well, but those modifications, for whatever reason, failed to stick.[9] Precisely how many spellings of modern English trace back to these anonymous compositors and their alterations, we can never know. But language historians agree that between irregular spellings that were settled in the lexicon by printers, as well as spellings that shifted because of an error or layout requirement, early printing houses are a major factor in the story of English's convoluted spelling code.

It's doubtful they ever thought about it in such terms, yet consider the power these typesetters had. Authors were obviously

shapers of orthography, especially those who wrote or translated the most popular books of the time, namely the Bible, *The
Canterbury Tales*, and the story of King Arthur. But it was the
typesetters who delivered words to readers in this new and in-
comparably authoritative-looking format. Print. If some or all
of the printers had used *s* and *h* to represent the sound *sh* in
every text they ever worked on, they could have done so, reliev-
ing future generations of the headaches induced by the likes of
nation, sugar, fissure, tenacious, and *charade*. If they'd wanted to,
or needed to for layout purposes, they could have nixed the final
-*e* from hundreds of other words. The effects of such alterations
remind me of the words of Mark Twain, who as a young man
worked as a typesetter: "The difference between the *almost*-right
word and the *right* word is really a larger matter—it's the difference between the lightning bug and the lightning."[10] He was talking about careful diction, yet this sense of profound consequence
spilling out of a seemingly subtle shift also applies to spelling. In
this case, the independently small but cumulatively significant
impact printers' adjustments, deletions, and substitutions had on
our language.

THE FIRST BOOK ever printed in English was published by a British merchant named William Caxton in 1475, give or take a year.
The book was Raoul Lefèvre's tales of the Trojan War, *Le recoeil des
histoires de Troyes*, and Caxton translated it himself—all seven hundred pages.[11] The landmark publication took place with no (known)
fanfare in the Belgian town of Bruges. This was a century prior to
Antwerp's rise as a printing center, and it was Caxton, before any
person on the planet, who first had to squeeze English's diverse dia-

lects, vocabulary, punctuation, and spelling into accessible, printed prose.

Modern-day Bruges is in many ways the same compact medieval city of canals and step-gabled brick buildings it was centuries ago. But the chocolatiers, weekend marching bands, and boats filled with tourists belie the city's past as a bustling center of commerce.[12] During the fourteenth and fifteenth centuries, Bruges was a nexus of international trade. Any number of languages could be heard within the city walls, as businessmen bought and sold goods, especially Flemish cloth, that would then be shipped to ports throughout the Continent and west to England.

After growing up in the southeast of England, Caxton apprenticed in London with a successful textiles merchant.* Sensing opportunity abroad, he decided to move to Bruges for a bigger piece of the action. He established an export business that would ultimately keep him away from England, mostly in Bruges, for the next thirty years. But he also spent some time in Germany, which is where he first learned about printing.[13]

As a savvy and well-traveled merchant who spoke many languages, Caxton would have had to have gone out of his way not to see Gutenberg's invention as a killer business opportunity. After purchasing three presses, he set to publishing his translation of *Lefèvre*. His customers were the local elite, English envoys, and nobility back in Britain.[14] The book did well, or at least well enough, and he soon moved back to England to set up shop near Westminster Palace. He brought with him his presses and a handful of trained

---

*He was probably born in the English town of Tenterden, although the town's only noticeable tribute to the father of English-language printing is an unimpressive pub called The William Caxton.

printers, presumably some of the same staff he had hired in Bruges. One of them, the marvelously named Wynkyn de Worde, went on to become one of England's most successful printers.

The atmosphere in the Westminster shop was one of frenzied excitement, perhaps comparable to that of a twenty-first-century tech start-up. Caxton possessed a technology no one in England had ever seen, and he had every reason to believe that books were going to impress and sell like crazy. Eager to maximize the efficiency of his operation and gain an edge over other publishing upstarts vying for a piece of the London market, Caxton worked to streamline the printing process by introducing a smaller type than had been previously used.[15] By 1480 he had published *The Canterbury Tales*, *Le Morte d'Arthur*, and a number of other works, assuring his position as the country's preeminent printer. When he died in 1492, Caxton had nearly one hundred published titles to his name.[16]

Caxton knew that he wouldn't be able to tame the dragon of English orthography; he would be lucky to keep it in a cage. "[C]omyn englysshe," he wrote, "that is spoken in one shyre varyeth from a nother."[17] When he wrote the word *right*, for instance, the chosen spelling corresponds to pronunciation of that period, which was more like "richt" (rhymes with "picked"). Caxton was approximating, though, for there was no established way to capture the sounds of words phonetically. "Certainly," he wrote, "it is hard to please every man by cause of diversity and change of language."[18] The word *might* alone has more than twenty variable spellings during this period of English evolution, including *myht*, *mihte*, *micte*, and *myght*.[19] As chief decider, Caxton had to shoot from the hip, knowing that while spelling could not be completely controlled, he was, in effect, seated at the controls.

Through verbose prologues, Caxton downplayed his power and tried to demonstrate humility. (Long prologues were common in those days, and the humble tone was meant to help sell books.) His de facto spelling policy, Caxton explained, was to record the "common terms that be daily used," preferring language that can be understood to "the old and ancient English." As he and other pioneering printers settled for best-estimate representations of spoken words, they in turn helped to crystallize spellings before anyone could really grasp that it was happening.[20] Yet readers who may have puzzled over how to pronounce Caxton's *right* didn't know how good they had it. The crevasse separating the sound of words from their written form was going to get wider still.

Caxton probably had little patience for matters of spelling. He was already busy translating, showing off his products to the king, and dealing with his employees and customers. As a result, his books include plenty of variable spellings. Is it *booke* or *boke* (for *book*), *goode* or *good*, *wyf* or *wyfe* (for *wife*), *hows* or *hous* (for *house*)? Caxton didn't say, and instead commits countless acts of orthographic flip-floppery, sometimes even on the same page of text.[21] The business of printing, after all, was about margins of pages and profit, not orthography dogma.

It would be another couple of generations after Caxton's death before spellings would truly settle, but the process began with his work, and some of his decisions, about spelling and about how to run his press operation, left a long-lasting imprint on the language. One historian suspects it was Caxton himself who transformed *gost* into *ghost*, in light of the fact that so much of his life was lived among Dutch-speaking and -writing people, but no one can say for sure.[22] However frequent they might have been, these word alterations were not problematic in and of themselves—it was their inconsistency that drove a deeper wedge between English spelling and pronunciation. If we always made the sound of a "g" with the letter combination of *gh*, that would be mildly inefficient, but at least it would be a regular rule that people learning English could easily follow: *ghastly, ghosts, ghettos*, and *aghast*. But no such luck. We also have *gas, goat, get*, and *against*, to say nothing of *gentle* and *gnarly, finger* and *single*.

The *gh* at the end of many modern words, however, like *dough, cough*, and *trough*, is actually an artifact not of Dutch orthographic tendencies, but of Norman distaste for the Middle English letter *yogh*, which looked like this: ⅈ. Yogh fell out of use around the end of the fifteenth century. At the time when Caxton began printing, the Middle English alphabet had another letter, the thorn, which looked like this: þ. But thorn didn't exist in German or Latin, which were the languages of the letter cases in Caxton's Western Europe orbit. There must have been a moment when Caxton, realizing there was no thorn available, decided to use the *t* and *h* in combination to create the þ sound. As professor Latre told me: "Caxton lost the beautiful thorn in Bruges." Just like that, a letter, gone.[*]

In addition to changes in lettering, there was a major pronunciation upheaval under way, which took place in an unusually compressed period of time, between Wycliffe's Bible and Caxton's first books—less than one hundred years. Scholars call it the Great Vowel Shift. No one knows what caused it, but the pronunciation of vowels in thousands of words underwent a relatively sudden change in quality. Whereas *name* was once pronounced like "nom" (rhymes with "bomb"), after the Great Vowel Shift it was and still is pronounced with a longer *a*, as in *game* or *aim*.

---

[*]Thorn was the last of the Old English holdouts. Eth, which looks like this, Đ, or this, ð, was gone by the fourteenth century. Ash (Æ or æ), as in Ælfric, is still used in languages like Norwegian and Danish, and we can still see it, or its shadow, in the British spelling of *mediaeval* (*mediæval*) and *archaeology* (*archæology*).

"There would have been grandparents and grandchildren who had trouble communicating with each other," Crystal told me. Listen to the different vowel sounds in *child/children*, *clean/cleanly*, and *hide/hid*.[23] Pronunciation was changing while many spellings remained anchored to the older forms. Why wasn't the spelling system amended to try to keep up with this new way of speaking English? "Because no one knew the pronunciation change was happening!" said Crystal. People didn't wake up one morning and notice that it was partly cloudy outside with a strong southwesterly breeze of shifting vowels. To people of medieval England, the process was natural. The English of Caxton's era was already a moving target, which meant pinning down an optimal and universally intelligible form for every word was a losing proposition. Publishing readable enough editions of bestselling texts, however, was very much a winning business proposition.

Caxton's spelling decisions, writes one author, did more to "regularize Standard English than his bestselling author, Chaucer."[24] While visiting Bruges, I stopped at a number of museums and cafés to ask people if they'd ever heard of Caxton. No one had. Not that Belgians should be blamed for failing to know about the first English printer, but for some reason I was wishing they did.

The printed pages coming off of Caxton's workshop presses gave people who could read English new and more material to consume. For one cross-section of society, that meant new opportunity to contemplate language and its relationship not just to knowledge, but also to cultural identity. Almost as soon as a more settled English orthography began spreading far and wide on the pages of printed texts, pundits began exhorting the importance of proper writing, and about the need for untangling the spelling code.

FIVE

VALIANT EXTERMINATORS OF DIALECTICAL VERMIN

I honor the Latin, but I worship the English[1]

Richard Mulcaster

B Y DAY'S END, THE Crystals and I had traveled some 160 miles through 500 years of English language history. From King Alfred through to Caxton and the advent of printing, we had covered, roughly speaking, Old and Middle English. "Now, if you want to blame people for spelling irregularity," said Crystal, "the next group is the sixteenth- and seventeenth-century scholars and spelling reformers." Between 1500 and 1750—from the arrival of printing to the publication of the first great dictionary—the English we now recognize as standard took shape. With it came something called correct spelling.

When linguists talk about language standards, they mean widely accepted conventions that facilitate smooth and easy communication, be it spoken, written, or signed. In short: norms. But during this next period in the evolution of English, something happened that had little to do with a scientific accounting of communication, and everything to do with culture and power. The guardians of England's class system co-opted the legitimate linguistic meaning of Standard English and transformed it into "correct English," a version of the language written and spoken as they saw fit. Over time, right and wrong ways to write and speak became indicators of education and class, distinguishing "us" from "them," the "haves" from the "have nots." In time, as more printed books circulated within the population, educated men began studying language, and in doing so found something they could obsesses over and tirelessly opine about: Words. Before long, they began spewing judgments about correct usage, grammar, speech, and spelling.

An ethic of accurate writing is at least as old as *Ælfric* and his tenth-century warning that careless text is equivalent to great evil. But correct English, and especially correct spelling, really only became a concern after the forces of printing helped establish a de facto standard language, and even then it was only the well-to-do who cared. Yet the arbiters of style did more than concern themselves with the state of English—they began copyediting it. When Caxton was working on his draft of *Le recoeil*, none other than the sister of the King of England suggested a red-pen change or two. He swiftly made the recommended corrections. If those edits conflicted with his sense of orthographic style, Caxton didn't say. Smart move. If you want your books to sell, best not to be on bad terms with the sovereign's sister.[2]

Yet without dictionaries, manuals, laws about language or the sister of the king ruling on every last word, against what measure would people assess the accuracy of words, spoken or written? A standard can't really exist without a certain degree of uniformity, and in the late Middle English period, the language still hadn't reached that level of widespread consistency.[3] English was undergoing a simultaneous upheaval and growth spurt in a relatively short period of time, with the Great Vowel Shift, a steady influx of word borrowings from French, Norse, Latin, and other languages, and changes wrought by the process of putting words to printed pages.

In the eyes of the men who saw themselves as stewards of culture and discourse, someone had to do something to end this lexicographical madness. "When people in the 1500s got turned on to Standard English," said Crystal, "spelling was really their top concern. Why? Because one would expect to see spelling idiosyncrasies in handwritten books, but not in printed texts." Everywhere they looked, language pundits found their countrymen mishandling the mother tongue. So they took matters into their own hands, hunting for linguistic blemishes, disagreements, and aesthetic horrors, and setting out to remedy them.

The first wave of deliberate spelling modification was the campaign to make words look more sophisticated, which at the time meant look less English. Phonetically inconsistent spelling wasn't much of a concern for this early generation of reformers—not nearly as much as etymology. English had regained respect thanks to the likes of Chaucer. But its renaissance was clipped, or at least delayed, by The Renaissance. A new era of science- and reason-minded scholars and writers felt a special affinity for Latin and Greek, sources for all of those cool new words, like *astronomy, politics, erosion, gravity,* and *insect.* At the same time they held steadfast to a lesser opinion of their native language. English, wrote essayist and philosopher Francis Bacon, will "play the bankrupts with the books."[4] Its perceived awkwardness and limitations, he believed, hindered intellectual endeavors. To minimize this effect, the more Greek or Latinate words or parts of words one crammed into one's writing, the more scholarly the final product.

As early as the fifteenth century, scribes and early printers performed cosmetic surgery on the lexicon. Their goal was to highlight the roots of words, whether for aesthetic pizzazz, homage to etymology, or both. The result was a slew of new silent letters.[5] Whereas *debt* was spelled *det, dett, or dette* in the Middle Ages, the "tamperers," as one writer calls them, added the *b* as a nod to the word's Latin origin, *debitum*.[6] The same goes for changes like the *b* in doubt (*dubium*), the *o* in *people* (*populous*), the *c* in *victuals* (victus), and the *ch* in *school* (*scholar*). *Schedule*, formerly *sedule* or *cedule*, was converted into the annoying *schedule*, again because of a love of Latin. In other cases, a misguided attempt to group words believed to be of similar origin led to spelling alterations that were confusing and etymologically incorrect. *Rime* or *ryme* acquired an *h* to make it look more like *rhythm*, and *delit* morphed into *delight* to bring it into line with *right* and *night*.[7] This was also about the time when *island* acquired an *s*, to make it look more like the Latin, *insula*.[*][8]

Greek was also held in high esteem, resulting in the addition

---

[*]*Island* has had an especially stormy history. Over the last millennium, it has been spelled: *iland, ealond, illond, yland, islelanders*, and, finally, *island*. The story of *aisle* is even more labyrinthine. With full credit to author Charles Earle Funke, it goes something like this: Originally from the Latin, *ala*, and then French, *ele*, for a passageway, in the fifteenth and sixteenth centuries English writers and printers began spelling it *ile*. But back then this was often how people spelled today's *isle*, as in "Gilligan's Isle." When *ile* as in landmass surrounded by water was dressed up into *isle*, the word meaning passageway got dressed up, too—*isle*. To try and remedy this confusion, eighteenth-century writers borrowed an *a* from French (*ele* had by then evolved into *aile* in France), but that created a new set of headaches because of the French *allée*, or *alley*. So the next and final fix was to just keep adding to the concoction, this time with an *s*. Voilà: *aisle*. (Charles Earle Funk, *Thereby Hangs a Tale: Stories of Curious Word Origins*, p. 8.)

of an *h* in words like *throne* and *theater*. And despite all the warring with the French, their language still managed to impress with its *je ne sais quoi*, which may explain why an "unhistorical *b*" was tacked on to the end of *limb*, *thumb*, and *crumb*, making them look similar to other words of French derivation—*bomb*, *plumb*, *tomb*, and *jamb*.[9] Around the same time, attempts to restore etymological integrity continued, and continued backfiring, as words like *sissors*, *coud*, and *ancor*, were turned into *scissors*, *could*, and *anchor*.[10] Things were getting out of hand.

Orthographic renovation was in one sense a whim-driven fad. Yet it was also an effective way to maintain the country's existing class hierarchy, making literacy less accessible to poorer and immigrant populations.[11] To get a handle on English now required more than an understanding of the sounds that corresponded to the letters of the alphabet. You also needed a mental database of foreign-derived roots and a seasoned awareness of irregular spellings, knowledge that well-educated people had but most others didn't. Without anyone expressly trying to make it so, English literacy was largely kept out of the everyman's reach.

Meanwhile, as British naval prowess, trade, and colonization expanded over the globe, words from abroad were rapidly absorbed into the English lexicon, perhaps as many as fifty thousand of them by the seventeenth century.[12] Pretty much anyone who played a part in this and later eras of globalization shares a bit of responsibility for the mess of English spelling, and likewise for the beauty of English's breadth. On the ships of the British East India Company and naval vessels, words from Hindi like *guru*, *dungaree*, *bungalow*, and *pundit* arrived into the language.[13] *Avocado*, *machete*, and *guitar* (Spanish), *bamboo* (Malay), *kiosk* (Turkish), *algebra* (Arabic), *parasite* (Greek), *cameo* (Italian), *curry* (Tamil), and so many more, from so many places.[14]

But like Caxton's crew of Dutch printers, the people bringing new words into English had to wing it when it came to spelling. Without a common strategy for turning foreign words into English ones, approximation ruled. *Curry* could have been *kurry*, *guitar* could have been *geetar*, *parasite* could have been *parisite* or *paricite*. That's not to say it was always a process of spelling alteration; in many instances, the words were unchanged or only slightly changed, and instead anglicized in the mouths of English speakers. *Brusque, cocoa, gazette, intrigue, canoe.*

Yet almost as soon as the emerging Standard English acquired all this bling, sounding a little more Italian here, trying to look more Latin there and showing off its souvenirs from abroad, along came a new crop of disgruntled intellectuals. Sixteenth-century culture editors began griping about how "counterfeit" words from "other tunges" were contaminating the "cleane and pure" English of Anglo-Saxon glory days. English was spiraling into "barbarousness" at the hands of vocabulary borrowings from abroad.[15] Alexander Gil, headmaster of the elite St. Paul's School when a boy named John Milton was a student, asserted that no language "will be found to be more graceful, elegant, or apt for the expression of every subtle thought than English."[16] To keep it that way, the language needed to be purged of foreign contaminants.

Not that that was even remotely possible. English, probably more so than any language on earth, "has a stunningly bastard vocabulary." Somewhere between 80 and 90 percent of all the words in the *OED* were born from other languages.[17] Old English, lest we forget, was already an amalgam of Germanic tongues, Celtic, and Latin, with pinches of Scandinavian and Old French influence as well. But in the eyes of sixteenth-century spelling reformers, this motley-from-the-get-go linguistic heritage was inconceivable, and they determined to return the language to the fantasyland of untarnished English.

A sixteenth-century London lawyer named John Hart believed he could rescue "our inglish toung" from further abuse by way of spelling reform.[18] Hart wanted to tackle the mismatch between spelling and pronunciation, and in 1569 he published a book laying out the details of an orthography overhaul. In *An Orthographie, conteyning the due order and reason, howe to write or paint thimmage of mannes voice, most like to the life of nature*,[19] Hart says English spelling has gotten so far out of whack that writing has become "a kind of ciphering."[20] He takes issue with inconsistent ways to create long versus short vowel sounds (the *o* sound in *moon* is long, but short in *foot*), and he can't stand the way we use the same letter to represent different sounds, such as the *g* in *gentry* versus the *g* in *gather*. To Hart, this inconsistency was the linguistic equivalent of fingernails on a chalkboard, as were superfluous letters—or what he would have called superfluous letters—like the *e* in *goode* (*good*), and the second *t* and the *e* in *sette* (today's *set*).[21]

To begin his English rescue mission, Hart tried to analyze the production of sounds based on the shape of the mouth and placement and movement of the tongue. (Some of his reformer successors drew meticulous diagrams of the operations of "the vocal organ."[22]) His idea was that by pinning down perfect pronunciation and then the spellings to represent it, he could once and for all weed out orthographic "vices and corruptions," nix useless letters, and replace every last inappropriately used letter in the lexicon.[23]

This audacious vision was common among Hart's fellow orthoepists, the then favored term describing the study of proper speech and its intersection with writing. A number of academics and English elite were drawn to the puzzle of orthography, worried about the widening spelling-pronunciation gap, and were game to engineer a fix.[24] Milton's teacher, Gil, was one of them. Isaac Newton, a few years before inventing calculus, scribbled in his journal about phonetics and the prospects of a universal human language.[25] Another spelling reform enthusiast, William Bullokar, published a sixty-four-thousand–word translation of *Aesop's Fables*, written in one of the trendy alternative spelling codes of the time. The title, as it appeared: *Aesopś Fablź.*[26]

Modern-day linguists appreciate the orthoepists. For one thing, both groups try to dig deep into the inner workings of language, from glottal stops and the descent of the larynx, to the vagaries of dialect in far-flung villages. But the more practical reason why the orthoepists matter so much to scholars today is because their work, despite its often erroneous and, as it turns out, bigoted, nature, their writings provide a window onto pronunciation of ages past.[27] A 1643 guide to orthography and "*the True-Writing of English*," for example, includes a list of homophones—that is, different words that sound the same. They're not homophones to most (American) listeners today, but they were then: *poles* and *Paul's*, *eat* and *ate*, *person* and *parson*, and *room* and *Rome.*[28]

To Hart and his ilk, spelling should reflect speech, and if that meant a total rewrite of the spelling code to date, so be it. It wasn't as crazy as it sounds. Printing had only been around for a few generations, which meant the public was still relatively accustomed to variable spelling. A revised system was not only warranted, the orthoepists believed, but also possible because the existing one was in its infancy. Once people saw how these recommended amendments would pull the language back from the brink of disaster, or something equally unattractive, of course they would adopt the changes. The time was ripe for reform.

But despite Hart's dedication, he couldn't muster much in the way of influential, let alone measurable, support. His scheme fell into the abyss of failed language reforms, as did Bullokar's *Aesops Fablź* and other orthographic innovations. Yet Hart did hit some of the right chords as far as the future direction of the language, and not just with *good* and *set*. Fifty years after his death in 1574, many of the word constructions Hart found most loathsome had vanished. In Shakespeare's *First Folio* (1623) there are 1,398 instances of *had* and only one of *hadde*.[29] Hart would have been happy with that.

Even if Hart had the power to institute his rewrite of the lexicon, whose speech patterns and accents would be the model for phonetic constructions? It's a tricky, if not impossible, question from a linguistics perspective, but to word pontiffs like Hart it was a no-brainer. The models of polite speech were and always should be the London, Oxford, and Cambridge elite. Hart even specified that speakers of this ideal English would not be found in places like "Newcastell upon Tine" and "Cornewale," which is to say out in the sticks.[30]

Far from being an historical factoid, this specification helped pave the way for future ideas about proper English speech, grammar, and spelling. When I lived in Japan, a number of Japanese friends deliberated between studying American English, generally considered to be easier for non-English speakers to learn because of pronunciation patterns, versus the "Queen's English," which they, and people all over the world, consider the more elegant style of speech. They didn't put it this way, but my Japanese friends' message was clear: Cowboys are cool and a vacation to Las Vegas is a must. But when it comes to proper English, everybody knows that the British are superior.

To Hart and the other orthoepists, correct English was the English of aristocrats like themselves. But their prescriptions for proper pronunciation failed to overcome an essential flaw in their plan to get everyone on the same speaking and writing page. It's one of the same problems that haunts modern-day spelling reformers and innovative spellers on Madison Avenue and in cyberspace. That is, phonetic to whom? Is it *schedule* as in "shejule" or "skejel"? "Boston" or "Baastin," "tomayto" or "tomahto"? Today, accents and dialects are generally valued as signs of regional identity, particularly in a world in which rare languages are dying out at a rate of roughly one every two weeks.[31] Sure, some people look down on or up to particular accents because of associated characteristics or stereotypes. From a linguistics perspective, though, accents are never better or worse, correct or incorrect. They just are, and their inevitability has a habit of dooming phonetic-based revisions of English orthography. We can't spell as we speak if we all speak differently.

While Hart was preaching nouveau spelling, still more scholars focused their ire on the matter of words' ethnic origins. Their goal was not merely to erect a fence around the English lexicon; they also wanted to raid safe houses of immigrant vocabulary and send those words packing. Opposition to foreign words was especially rowdy at Kings College in Cambridge, where a sixteenth-century Provost named John Cheke worried that "borrowing of other tunges" would gradually render English bankrupt.[32] Cheke introduced new spellings under the guise of returning Englishness to English. He lobbied for changes such as eradicating many silent final *e*'s and implementing double *a*'s to indicate long-*a* pronunciation: *aancient*, *waav*, *aag*, and *taap*.[33] And Alexander Gil continued railing against the incorporation of Latinate words and other linguistic impurities, calling them "evil-sounding magpies and owls" of unfavorable birth that only served to injure words and contaminate the English language.[34]

But not all language mavens of old were quite so livid. One in particular demonstrated a more realistic grasp of the linguistic universe, while still hoping to narrow the gap between orthography and pronunciation. Richard Mulcaster was head teacher of the prestigious Merchant Taylor's school in London. He was as neurotic about systematic stewardship of English as Hart, but his approach was one of realpolitik modification. In his 1582 treatise on education called *The Elementarie*, Mulcaster acknowledges inconsistencies within English orthography, but concludes that "custom" had carried regional pronunciation so far out into the ocean of lexical diversity that implementation of a wholly new phonetic system would never work. With this recognition, Mulcaster earns the title of history's first spelling reformer who tried to balance a vision for improvement with a sense of practicality. You can't fold or start a new game, Mulcaster might have said, but you can improve your hand.

To make his play, Mulcaster made a list of over 8,500 words as part of his guide to teach students to write and speak properly. A complete return to the simpler orthography of Anglo-Saxon times may not have been feasible, but that didn't mean it was impossible to rectify many contradictory spelling rules and forms.[35] Like Hart, Mulcaster went after apparently needless letters and reshuffled others, but he was more selective: *flag* (from *flagge*), *frog* (from *frogge*), *fin* (from *finn*), *fort* (from *forte*), and *flame* (from the Middle English *flaume* or *flaumbe*).[36] As it turned out, his sense of direction was just shy of clairvoyant. More than half of the spelling refinements Mulcaster made match regular spellings today, and many others differ only nominally.[37] That's not to say we spell them his way because he told us to, but the whittling he called for was on the mark.

* * *

ONE OF THE challenges for anyone plugging for top-down spelling reform is how to unseat existing spelling practice, especially when that practice still varies from printer to printer. Say you had a good idea for changing the language, even if it was just the deletion of one letter from one word, but you just *knew* it was superior to other possible spellings for that word. How would you spread the word and make it stick? Maybe you'd start by composing a manifesto explaining the superiority of this new construction. But how would you broadcast it in such a way that other writers would adopt the new spelling, printers would type it and readers would come to expect the word spelled your way, over the old way, always? If you had a new idea for a rule adjustment in baseball, you could write to Major League Baseball. If you had a suggested improvement to fifth-grade mathematics instruction, you could bring it up with the Department of Education. You may get stonewalled by bureaucracy, but you know where to turn.

Sixteenth- and seventeenth-century language shapers had no institutional authority to turn to for help in establishing a standard that was up to their standards. The French have, or try to have, a centralized, "unchallengeable" authority for their language.[38] *L'Académie Française*, established in 1634, makes rulings about the language, and French speakers and the language are supposed to respond and behave accordingly. (The forty academy members are known as The Immortal Forty.) The Italians have an academy as well, and a few times in recent history the German and Dutch governments have made official tweaks to their tongues, most recently in the 1990s, by way of government edict. The effort in Germany caused considerable turmoil, with many influential groups and newspapers refusing to adopt the new "rules."

As modern English was taking shape, a handful of seventeenth-century English tastemakers looked across the Channel with envy at *L'Académie Française*, and set out to steer the USS *English* back on course by way of an academy for English. When England's Royal Society was launched in the 1660s to direct and promote scientific research, one of its top agenda items was to try to improve the English language. It wasn't real science, but giving it the trappings of formal investigation helped conjure credibility. The campaign would start with a committee, of course. From there, the committee would select eminent men to issue decrees about such-and-such aspect of the language that would then become the final word.

One man who was ready and willing to take on this responsibility was the distinguished poet-playwright-essayist John Dryden, whose body of work included the tragedy "Tyrannick Love" and "Aurengzebe."*[39] Dryden outlined an argument for an academy to help fix the language in place. Falling back on the favorite descriptor of the age, he lamented that English had descended into a "barbarous" state because there was "not so much as a tolerable dictionary or a grammar" anywhere to be found. Like many intellectuals, Dryden revered Chaucer, and worried about mutations in the language that had taken place during the roughly 250 years since *The Canterbury Tales* had been written. Parts of the masterpiece were already difficult to comprehend, and Dryden blamed language change. If English continued to morph willy-nilly, the great works—perhaps Dryden's included—faced future incomprehensibility and thus obsolescence. That was, unless the captains of English could set an anchor.[40]

---

*All of these renaissance men, almost by definition, have hyper-hyphenated descriptors. No high-society figure back then was just a poet, just a pundit, or just a translator.

Putting aside for a moment the impossibility of locking any language in time and form, Dryden's idea faced an additional hurdle: William Shakespeare. The Bard had, and would continue to have, a catastrophic effect on efforts to impose order on the language. Together with his contemporaries of the late 1500s and early 1600s, Shakespeare went ballistic with linguistic experimentation. There was a pyrotechnic playfulness with which Shakespeare and other writers broke rank from language constraints. He was, as he put it, a "man on fire for new words," wielding and augmenting the lexicon with equal mastery.[41]

Shakespeare is credited with coining more than two thousand words, infusing thousands more existing ones with electrifying new meanings and forging idioms that would last for centuries.* "A fool's paradise," "at one fell swoop," "heart's content," "in a pickle," "send him packing," "too much of a good thing," "the game is up," "good riddance," "love is blind," and "a sorry sight," to name a few. Dryden, quilling some fifty years after Shakespeare's heyday, detested language change and decried the drift from Chaucerian English. He seems to have been oblivious to, or in denial of, Chaucer's own playfulness with the language of his day, while turning a blind eye to colossal changes brought about by Shakespeare.

By the time Shakespeare was writing, the majority of English spellings were either settled or were on their way to being settled. In that sense, Shakespeare can't really be considered a member of the nuclear family of spelling reformers. But he had a huge impact on

---

*When looking at word innovation, linguists distinguish between word and lexeme, which is the base of a word. *Take, took, taken, takes,* and *taking* are all forms of the single lexeme, *take.* Shakespeare created more than 2,000 lexemes, possibly many more. (David Crystal personal interview, September 2007.)

orthography. For one thing, his lexical innovations further stymied the quest for stability. If the boundaries of Standard English weren't blurred enough already, all the new words, usages, and expressions springing from Shakespearian and Elizabethan English only made the reform more challenging. He also usurped Chaucer as the gold standard. On a post-Shakespearian earth, his name would forever be associated with English of unparalleled sophistication and elegance.

For a drink in the Bard's honor, David and Hilary took me to The Dirty Duck, their favorite watering hole in Shakespeare's hometown of Stratford-upon-Avon. "Language is people," Crystal told me as we stared out at the River Avon. Words are not the flesh of thought entirely, for we also think in pictures, sounds, tastes, smells, and feelings. But words are an essential part of the flesh of society and cultural intercourse. They are products of human innovation, folly, power, preference, and change. For that reason, correct English is nothing more than a phantom. That doesn't make English any less expansive and glorious, but the idea that there is clearly a right or a wrong way to go about the business of pronunciation, grammar, or even spelling, flies in the face of language's true machinations.

Not everyone is hunky-dory with this realist take. To a remarkable degree, people view words, as well as grammar and punctuation rules, as if they were jewels handed down from God by way of sixth-grade teachers—that there is simply a right way to wield a comma, spell *rhubarb*, or place modifiers. Crystal and most linguists take the view that language is always changing and that the purpose of linguistics is to describe how words and rules are used, not to tell people how to use them. Other people believe that the traditions of language that they learned in school exist for a reason, and therefore should be taught and enforced. The technical label for this contrasting approach is descriptivism versus prescriptivism.

The more benign form of prescription in linguistics doesn't really bug anyone. It lays out general rules for grammar and spelling, which help to make written language as widely and easily intelligible as possible. Where the sparks begin to fly is out on the periphery, where prescription inevitably seeps into matters of taste, political correctness, and socially acceptable usage. Or, as Crystal puts it: The absolutist, "zero-tolerance attitudes that start to sound like George W. Bush." These hard-line prescriptivists, these "valiant exterminators of dialectical vermin," to borrow a phrase from Benjamin Ide Wheeler, believe in a clear dividing line between proper and improper language. They believe it's the responsibility of educators, academics, writers, and editors to direct the use of language so as to inoculate future texts from sentences that end in prepositions and prevent high-schoolers from ever saying "between you and I" when they mean "between you and me."

To descriptivists, "between you and I" and "between you and me" are both possible. Both deliver the desired nugget of information without a hitch and the fact is people nowadays are using both expressions. Strict prescriptivists in turn decry this type of change as evidence of further mangling of the language, waving copies of Strunk and White's *The Elements of Style* to assert the correctness of their views about correctness. (That "little book," writes linguist Geoffrey Nunberg, "has done more than anything else to persuade people that the whole subject of usage can be reduced to a few pithy maxims . . . "[42]) Disciplined use of language, they argue, makes for clarity of expression, benefiting writer and reader alike. Descriptivists then fire back to say they honor clarity too, but want to distinguish between phony and legitimate rules that ensure it.

A grammatical experiment that confuses a sentence doesn't

do much good, and most everyone agrees that rules to help avoid such confusion make sense. With spelling, though, the assertion is shakier. When people confuse *dam* and *damn* or *ingenious* and *ingenuous*, usage referees are right to throw a penalty flag. These are two different words that mean two different things. This kind of slipup invites confusion, as do other homophones, like *compliment* and *complement*, *stationary* and *stationery*, *booze* and *boos*, *pedal* and *peddle*, and so many others. But to insist that using *supercede* instead of *supersede* necessarily bolsters clarity feels like a stretch. What about *hair-brained* versus *hare-brained*, *straitjacket* and *strait-laced* versus *straight-jacket* and *straight-laced*, or even—deep breath now—*through* versus *thru*?[43] These variable constructions may grate on one's sense of aesthetic, much in the same way many people get nauseous when they hear the word *incentivise*. But does that make them wrong? Do these misspellings to some, alternative spellings to others, truly make a sentence less intelligible?

When asked to comment about the standard language, Crystal usually talks about grammar and punctuation—they are more often the topic of debate. Yet the response he often experiences when discussing grammar can also apply to spelling. Crystal has found that nudging the public away from devotion to an imagined notion of pure language is no easy task. "People who never let themselves get pushed around in other walks of life" bow down to language rules and rule enforcers.[44] I would have to agree. While researching or casually talking about this book project, I frequently met people who "detest" poor spelling and "can't stand" to see truncated renditions of words in text messages or emails. It's as if being a spelling neocon is somehow cool.

As linguist and author Anthony Burgess once put it: "When we think we are making an objective judgment about language, we are often merely making a statement about our prejudices." In media and lecture appearances, Crystal is often cast as the wet blanket—the guy who wants to snuff out the cheeky fun derived from policing the language and faithfully maintaining traditions of yesteryear. Crystal is the opposite of a curmudgeon, yet he ends up sounding like one anyway, telling people that whining about bad English doesn't make sense. The irony of course, is that it's the pundits who are adhering to pretensions, while descriptivists like the sixty-six-year-old Crystal point out that what we think of as Correct English is scientifically nonsensical, has roots in classist and even racist thinking, and runs counter to the experimental, playful, and conversational language of not-too-shabby writers like Chaucer and Shakespeare.

This tension is hardly limited to ivory tower settings. Get people talking about language or spelling standards, and they'll inevitably bring up the 1990s brouhaha over Ebonics, whatever their recollection of it may be. Combining the words *ebony* and *phonics*, the term is used to describe the variety of English known as African-American Vernacular English (AAVE). At the end of 1996, the outgoing school board in Oakland, California passed what was in fact an unremarkable resolution stating that AAVE is a separate language from English (it isn't). Somehow, the resolution was misinterpreted as a call for Ebonics to be taught alongside the Standard English curriculum.

A brief culture war ensued, racist overtones and all. Some observers were convinced that urban language posed a threat to the language of—that's right—Shakespeare. Linguists quietly told anyone willing to listen that Ebonics isn't slang or corrupted English, that it is no less grammatically sophisticated than the English of history's literary giants, and that language variation is normal, inevitable, and healthy. But their message was drowned out by the uproar.[45] Ebonics was an affront to the clean and pure mother tongue.

"At the heart of linguistics," Crystal once wrote, "is the distinction between 'grammatical' and 'ungrammatical,' between 'acceptable' and 'unacceptable.' It is the boundary line which attracts all the arguments."[46] In the most recent decades of this battle, spelling has avoided the kind of attention that punctuation and grammar receive. People don't think much about it, in large part because most of us prefer to see words spelled in a consistent and familiar form. Misspelled words confuse and look "bad," which is, or has usually been, close enough to saying that they're "incorrect."

They are, kinda. Yet the boundary between conventionally accepted linguistic norms and this cultural thing we call "correct spelling" is blurrier and more fluid than we realize, certainly more so than a schoolteacher's harsh red pen suggests. An average collegiate-edition dictionary of one hundred thousand words can have variable spellings for up to 25 percent of its entries, when you include capitalizations and hyphenated words—think *dark-room* v. *darkroom*, *absinthe* v. *absinth*, *flower pot* v. *flower-pot*, and *Bubonic Plague* v. *bubonic plague*.[47]

Hyphens are so widely mismanaged, misappropriated, and misunderstood that in 2007 the powers that be behind the *OED* decided to eliminate some sixteen thousand of them, mostly ones that once linked compound nouns. As reported by the *New York Times*, "Some [words], like 'ice cream,' 'fig leaf,' 'hobby horse,' and 'water bed,' have been fractured into two words, while many others, like 'bumblebee,' 'crybaby,' and 'pigeonhole,' have been squeezed into one."[48]

A forty-five-year veteran of the publishing industry recently wrote a book about "bad English," in which he clarifies many oft-confused snippets of spelling and usage. My favorite: "*Supersede*. This is the correct spelling. There is no such word as *supercede*," he writes.[49] What would happen, though, if someone dared to say that *supercede* is a word? It sure looks like a word. *Recede, antecede*, and *precede* are real words, and readers will easily understand the intended meaning of *supercede* despite the "error." Today, my current version of Microsoft Word gives the *c-spelled* version a red squiggly. But plug *supercede* into a Google search, and (as of today), you'll get some 722,000 hits, compared to 2.4 million for *supersede*. And with the former entry, you won't be asked: "Did you mean: **Supersede**." So now what?*

Merriam-Webster's 2008 *Collegiate New World Dictionary* includes a handful of new words with alternative spellings, such as *pescatarian/pescetarian* (someone who doesn't eat meat but does eat fish), *za/'za* (for pizza), and *ta-da/ta-dah* (as in, voilà!). The inclusion of more than one acceptable spelling, a Merriam-Webster lexicographer told me, is necessary because the words are new enough that they haven't yet settled. There's no algorithm for determining whether a spelling has or hasn't settled, only the expert judgment of lexicographers. Yet someday, those words will, or probably will, settle. This happens because the media and publishers make spelling choices, and because teachers start telling their students that *pescatarian* is wrong but *pescetarian* is right, or the other way around.

Magnify those judgment calls over the population of all teachers, writers, and lexicographers over a year or decade, and then multiply that by all the words they weigh in on, and the taste-driven reality of

---

*In 1950, a National Spelling Bee contestant was dinged for spelling *supercede*, only to be allowed back into the match after the judges conferred and decided that both *supercede* and *supersede* are acceptable spellings. (James Maguire, *American Bee*, p.78)

orthography evolution becomes that much clearer. As for the students writing *pescatarian* for a teacher who expects *pescetarian*, there's now a tantalizing second option to consider before accepting the conclusion that you've made a mistake: Explain your feelings about *pescetarianism* on blogs and in Facebook conversations that happen to reach ten million seafood-eating English speakers and enlist them in an orthographic coup. If Shakespeare were around today, he'd probably say of the two different spellings: The teacher's a knave. Use 'em both!

UNFORTUNATELY FOR JOHN Dryden, his attempt to establish a home for an oligarchy of prescriptivists flopped almost upon conception. It may have been that people finally started to envision a price tag for this undertaking, or question how a language academy would actually work. But the even more likely reason why the cause was so quickly dropped was the bubonic plague, which broke out (again) in the spring of 1665. Anyone who could flee London did. If that wasn't enough suffering and destruction wrought by Nature, the following year brought the Great Fire, further hindering the efforts of privileged men to convene a high court of the language.[50]

A generation later, Daniel Defoe, author of *Robinson Crusoe* and *Moll Flanders*, published an article titled "On Academies." It was high time, Defoe proposed to King William III, for a governing body to "advance the so much neglected Faculty of Correct Language, to establish Purity and Propriety of Stile, and to purge it of all the Irregular Addition that Ignorance and Affectation have introduc'd; and all those Innovations in Speech, if I may call them such, which some Dogmatic Writers have the Confidence to foster upon their Native Language, as if their Authority were sufficient to make their own Fancy legitimate."[51] In other words, Your Highness, wannabe language authorities are acting as if they possess the very power that should belong to people like me.

By 1650, printing conventions were spreading, which meant spelling variability was diminishing. Spelling guides for children began to hit bookstore shelves, sold alongside guides to manners and speech, thus furthering the association of proper spelling with proper living. The gap between how people spoke and how their words were represented orthographically was as screwy as ever. But the new books, grammar guides, and starter dictionaries provided at least some measure against which one could judge whether a spelling was correct—and by extension judge the speller.

For centuries, literacy was an essential dividing line between classes because only people of premium pedigree were educated. As books, knowledge, and education became more widespread, however, the new tool for distinguishing "us" from "them" was proper language—speech, writing, and spelling. Acceptance of variable spelling was waning, and correct spelling emerged not merely as something to aspire to for the sake of clear communication based on linguistic norms, but also as a prerequisite for acceptance within the upper echelons of English society.

Not that access was easily attainable. Newly published etiquette guides and spelling books weren't enough to clean up what upper-class gentlemen perceived to be dirty English. *Gulliver's Travels* author Jonathan Swift felt the country was engulfed in a monsoon of uncouth English. Exasperated, he revived the academy idea once again. A cousin of Dryden's, Swift didn't permit his Irish roots to interfere with his myopic view of language correctness and his conviction that "corruptions in our language have not at least equaled the refinements of it."[52] In his "Proposal for Correcting, Improving and Ascertaining the English Tongue," he blames almost every literate person in the country for the decrepit state of the language, including spelling reformers, playwrights, poets and, "the young academics, who . . . borrow the newest Sett of Phrases, and if they take Pen into their Hands, all the odd words they have picked up in a Coffee-House or a Gaming Ordinary [gambling-house], are produced as Flowers of Style."[53]

Swift's disdain for language change was all-consuming and, in a twisted way, impressive. Clipped words, as in *taxi* from *taxicab*, *bus* from *omnibus*, and *rep* for *reputation* were repulsive.* Apostrophe-enabled contractions like *disturb'd* and *rebuk'd* were despicable. Chic new words like *banter, shuffling, bully,* and *sham* were shameful. Spelling as we speak—*sartinly* for *certainly,* for instance—would destroy etymology, he believed, and if such a practice were permitted, over time "whoever hath been used to plain *English*, will hardly know them by sight." Swift wanted to pull back on the reins. "I see no absolute Necessity why any Language should be perpetually changing," he wrote. Through the effective influence of an academy, Swift, like others before him, believed he could whip the language and its speakers into shape.[54]

The language academy was never much more than a long shot. As Crystal once put it, the English attitude toward language seems to be more laissez-faire than that of continental Europeans. One contemporary of Swift's who wasn't drinking the Kool-Aid suggested that while Swift was shooting for the moon with his academy, he might as well set up institutions to engineer the Grand Elixir and develop a perpetual motion machine.[55]

By the eighteenth century, if the aspiring academicians had any

---

Taxicab is in fact a double contraction, from the French, *taximeter cabriolet* (Charles Earle Funk, *Thereby Hangs a Tale: Stories of Curious Word Origins,* p.50).

lingering hope for an English language Security Council, that hope was silenced for good by Samuel Johnson. One of that century's titanic scholars, Johnson saw the French academy's inability to control the French language as unassailable evidence that a British academy would never fly: "We live in an age in which it is a kind of publick sport to refuse all respect that cannot be enforced," wrote Johnson. "The edicts of an English academy would probably be read by many, only they might be sure to disobey them."[56] The academy was dead. Yet in an ironic turn, it was Johnson who would give the correctness demagogues a device for establishing language authority without the need for authoritarian oversight: an illustrious dictionary.

Johnson was born in 1709. A revered writer-critic-essayist-lexicographer, he did most of his work in a London apartment just off of Fleet Street, the epicenter of the English printing industry. But his hometown was a place called Lichfield. On the second day of our journey, the Crystals and I made our way there. "On we go," said David, as we walked to the yellow three-story house in the center of town, "to the other end of Standard English."

Johnson's father was a bookseller, and it's a safe bet that a childhood surrounded by words was advantageous for the man who would go on to write the most comprehensive dictionary the world had ever seen. Three flights of rickety stairs inside the Samuel Johnson Birthplace Museum lead visitors to a room displaying an early edition of his most famous work, artifacts such as a wooden portable writing desk, and books from his family collection—zippy titles like *The Preternatural State of Animal Humors Described by the Sensible Qualities* and *An Impartial View of the Truth of Christianity; with the History of the Life and Miracles of Apollonius Tyanæus, containing.* . . . Taking a quill in my hand at the museum, I needed three dips in the ink jar just to write out a single word of unexceptional length: spelling. "Think of the slog," said Crystal, referring to Johnson's nine years of writing and editing *A Dictionary of the English Language*. It would have been a monumental feat even with more efficient writing technology.*

"If you're going to be a dictionary writer, you have to be of a certain temperament," said Crystal. Johnson suffered from scrofula, a skin disease usually caused by an infection in the lymph nodes. It left him deaf in one ear. As a young man, he didn't have clear career designs. He studied at Oxford for a stint, but had to retreat home to Lichfield because of financial problems. "Poverty followed him like a shadow," wrote his biographer and friend James Boswell. Johnson started out as a teacher, with limited success and apparently less satisfaction, before trying his hand as a writer. Even after he had established a solid reputation, though, money was always an issue. When Johnson was offered an advance of £1,575 in 1746 to produce a dictionary, he said yes despite failing to secure further funding from a patron, as was common practice in those days.

Many people mistakenly credit Johnson with writing the first English dictionary. That achievement belongs to a man named Cawdrey, who, 150 years before Johnson, published *A Table Alphabetical*. It was only 144 pages and defined some 2,500 difficult words; the rest people were just supposed to know.[57] With its emphasis on boosting vocabulary, Cawdrey's book is a lot like modern-day titles that help you pump up your word arsenal before attacking the SAT or waging war in the corporate world.

Other dictionaries followed Cawdrey's, but by the mid-

---

*Titles back then were not short. The full title of Johnson's epic work is: *A Dictionary of the English Language: In Which the Words Are Deduced from Their Originals, and Illustrated in Their Different Significations by Examples from the Best Writers. To Which Are Prefixed a History of the Language and an English Grammar.*

eighteenth century Johnson could see that English and its speakers needed something better. The language "was in a state of anarchy," he wrote. "The time for discrimination seems to be now come. Toleration, adoption and naturalization have run their lengths. Good order and authority are now necessary."[58] He would apply a whole new level of scrutiny to lexicography, revealing that much of the complexity and magic of the language was buried within the nuance and flexibility of seemingly easy words. For the word *go* he recorded sixty-eight different definitions, in an entry covering three pages.

In comprehensiveness and heft, *A Dictionary of the English Language* wasn't just unmatched; it forever changed the definition of dictionary. It contains 43,000 entries written out in some 3 million words with 118,000 quotations to illustrate usage. It's five and one-half times longer than Tolstoy's *War and Peace*.[59] The two brown leather-bound books are as long as the distance from your elbow to your fingertips, and about four inches thick. The beige pages are soft and speckled in places with tiny marks, almost like grease stains, that are in fact a tiny (and harmless) mold that commonly grows on antique paper because it has never been bleached.

In the attic of Johnson's Lichfield home, I flipped to some definitions. *To Spell* is "to write with the proper letters." *Correct*, from Latin, means "revised or finished with exactness; free from faults." *Orthography* is "the art or practice of spelling," and for this one Johnson includes a quotation from Swift: "In London they clip their words after one manner about the court, another in the city, and a third in the suburbs; all which reduced to writing, would entirely confound orthography." For *rhubarb*, Johnson turns to Shakespeare for illustration. "A medicinal root slightly purgative referred by botanists to the dock. '*What rhubarb, senna, or what purgative drug would scour these English hence?*'" asked Macbeth.

When he started, Johnson set his sights on removing "spots of barbarity impressed" deeply in the language. To proscribe English in its entirety, he knew he had to level judgments, especially about spelling. In his preface to the *Dictionary* Johnson writes: "When all the words are selected and arranged, the first part of the work to be considered is the orthography," in which there remains "great uncertainty among the best cricks: nor is it easy to state a rule by which we may decide between custom and reason . . . " One rule he could firmly state, however, was that English words shouldn't end with *c*. As a result, his *Dictionary* is filled with the likes of *musick, critick, attick, epick, tropick, chaotick, publick,* and even *publickly*. (This was one of Johnson's more noticeable miscalculations of "custom"; within a decade or two, most people were omitting the tacked-on *k*.[60]) Johnson was also a man of opinions and at times they worked their way into the *Dictionary*. ("*Ruse*: A French word neither elegant nor necessary.")

But Johnson's overall strategy for handling variable spellings was, at least on paper, to "make no innovation without a reason sufficient to balance the inconvenience of change; and such reasons I do not expect often to find. All change is of itself an evil, which ought not to be hazarded but for evident advantage . . . " The contracted spelling *thro*, for example, he thought was crafted "by barbarians from *through*." And he did occasionally give in to the urge to innovate, as was the case with *dispatch*. Johnson spells it *despatch*, despite the fact that in all his source quotations it's spelled with an *i*.[61] For the most part, though, his dictionary wasn't about putting a personal stamp on the language. He wanted to get it down, all of it in one book, so as to solidify the lexicon and do away with (much) inconstancy, which he felt was "a mark of weakness" that hurt "the reputation of our tongue." Johnson's *Dictionary* promised to lock words in place in a manner Swift and other preservationists could have only dreamed.

But nine years spent trying to read, define, and edit forty-three thousand words can change a man. Johnson came to realize just how impossible it was, and is, to pin down a language. "That our language is in perpetual danger of corruption cannot be denied; but what prevention can be found?" Even his dictionary couldn't provide sufficient reinforcement; the language remained unstable and English purity, orthographic or otherwise, was as elusive as ever. By the end of his language odyssey, Johnson had learned that the lexicographer's responsibility wasn't to decide upon and shape, "but to register the language," documenting how people have "hitherto expressed their thoughts."[62]

As for orthographic revolution, Johnson, writing some two hundred years after Mulcaster and company, was dealing with a far more settled English spelling system. True, Shakespeare was explosively inventive and loanwords, as well as new words springing from scientific discoveries, were growing the language. For a test-drive of some new words from Johnson's *Dictionary*, take a spin with *ophiophagous* ("Serpent-eating"), *clodpate* ("A stupid fellow; a dolt; a thickscull"), and *garlericulate* ("Covered as with a hat").[63] Yet usage habits were crystallizing rapidly, as Mulcaster had even noted two centuries prior. By 1800, English orthography was buried deep in irregular spelling soil, with tens of thousands of words now frozen into a shape that would preserve the fissure between the sounds of spoken language and their representation in writing. Johnson's impact was really one of cementing, not changing, spelling forms, lining them up in the pages of a supremely authoritative reference book. From Johnson's time forward, spelling questions or disputes were easy to resolve. How do you spell a word? Just look it up.

SIX

OUTLAW ORTHOGRAPHY

> Every changed spelling now in general—whether for the better,
> as fish from fysshe, dog from dogge, or for the worse, as rhyme
> from rime, delight from delite—was once the overt act of a
> single writer, who was imitated at first by a small minority.[1]
>
> *From* Handbook of Simplified Spelling *(1920) New York*

JOHN MORSE PULLED THE handle opening a red filing drawer, then picked out an index card. The drawers are fire-resistant, but the truly taboo word at the editorial offices of Merriam-Webster, Inc. is water (" \wo·tər, 'wä-\ *noun 1a:* the liquid that descends from the clouds as rain . . . "). Water damage could do a lot more harm to the collection of seventeen million citations stored in those files than most fires could, which is why there are no sprinklers in the building at 47 Federal Street in Springfield, Massachusetts. Charred cubicles, computers, reference books, and personal effects: no big deal. Water-logged, moldy, and illegible citations: a lost treasure.

Morse, Merriam-Webster's president and publisher, read the typed contents of the card. The word was *whack*, as in, *whacked his head on the low ceiling.* The handful of cards stored just in front of or behind this one identify other meanings of the same word, such as the Tony Soprano-esque, *to whack a rival gangster,* or the (currently slang), *take a whack at it,* meaning to try or attempt. Next we leafed through a stack of pages for a forthcoming dictionary. Each page has a bunch of pencil marks to identify needed changes. "We also have everything on computer of course," said Morse. "But a lot of this is still done by hand." As Morse flipped through a few sheets, I spotted an *AF* in the margin. Anglo-French, he explained. A new byte of derivation information bound for future editions of the dictionary.

The forty lexicographers and editors at Merriam-Webster are charged with wrangling new words and usages, and adding them to the company's ever-growing physical and virtual accounts of the English language. The method for dictionary compilation, known as reading and marking, has remained mostly unchanged since 1857, when a Scotsman named James Murray began recruiting people to mine sample text—primarily books at first, but source material later expanded to include magazines, leaflets, newspapers, office documents, whatever—for examples of new words or novel senses of older ones. For each word or usage, readers sent in a card detailing the citation. Murray then collated them for a project he was working on called the *Oxford English Dictionary.*[*]

Technology has blown open the universe of reading material. The Merriam-Webster staff uses hundreds of Internet resources, archives from LexisNexis, and the company's own corpus, a body of accumulated text that contains around one hundred million words.

---

[*]Samuel Johnson's method for compiling the dictionary was essentially the same, but he didn't solicit outside help the way Murray did.

That's what it takes to continually track new words, meanings, and variant spellings. I asked about all the writing in cyberspace, where a quick Google search will yield nearly fifty thousand hits for a "misspelled" query like *rubarb*. Not all writing is source material, said Morse. "There's still a prescriptivist tradition in this country. People get jumpy when you talk of changing the language," which is another way to say that every last spelling variant on the Web doesn't necessarily qualify as an alternative spelling in a grand old dictionary.

But jumpy constituents or not, the language does change, which is why Morse introduced me to Jim Lowe. A forty-year Merriam-Webster veteran and, in Morse's words, a "born definer," Lowe is the point person who, after scouring the landscape of the lexicon, compiles the short list of new words and their spellings for the *Collegiate New World Dictionary*, which is revised annually. During my visit, Lowe was finalizing the list of new words for the 2008 edition. Please welcome not only *za/'za* and *pescatarian/pescetarian*, but also *podcast*, *kiteboarding*, *cyberterrorism*, *subprime*, *air-kiss*, and a few dozen others.

If some of these words don't sound brand new, that's because the unwritten rule of lexicography is that words need a little time to settle. That way, editors can distinguish between a letter string that was briefly well known but then faded out, and a recently coined construction that's here to stay and can safely be called a word. People were using *google* (2001) as a verb for a couple of years before the *OED* or Merriam-Webster put it in the dictionary, and the same is true for invented words throughout the ages, from *caucus* (1763) to *scrunchie* (1988). Some words rapidly accumulate ample citations to convince lexicographers that they're widely used and here to stay (*AIDS* is a somber example). Other words make their presence known in the lexicon, but it's a toss-up between two spellings, such as *pescetarian* versus *pescatarian*. And then there are the thousands of words for which a spelling dispute was never resolved: *blond/ blonde, disk/disc, gray/grey, leaped/leapt, savory/savoury, woolen/ woollen, cauldron/caldron, douse/dowse.*

Morse and other editors review each year's new additions, but the heavy lifting in terms of defining meanings is left to Lowe. In choosing to call Lowe a born definer, Morse was paying his colleague lexicography's ultimate compliment. It was the *OED*'s Murray who had described dictionary legend Noah Webster as "a born definer of words."

DRIVING SOUTH THROUGH the Connecticut River Valley, Morse and I passed colonial homes and fields of corn and tobacco, before reaching the run-down commercial strips of West Hartford. A few minutes later we turned into the parking lot next to a barn-red building that now hosts a small museum and visitor center. Inside, we met the museum director and gathered around the hearth of the original eighteenth-century farmhouse to learn about the childhood of a spelling rebel.

Noah Webster's family worked a ninety-acre farm. They raised sheep, cows, and horses, and grew corn, tobacco, squash, artichoke, flax, and hay.[2] Noah senior served as justice of the peace for the village of West Hartford. He wasn't a judge, but people called him "Judge Webster" anyway.[3] Noah's great-great-grandfather had been governor of Connecticut in 1656, but roots didn't guarantee Noah a position of repute within revolutionary-era America.[4] All but the wealthiest boys growing up in the 1760s stopped attending school by the time they were teenagers, their contributions on the farm too valuable to spare. Noah and his four siblings hoed and harvested during the day, and at night churned butter, pulled wool, and beat flax to make linen.

The farmhouse had little in the way of belongings other than farm tools, kitchen utensils, and a Bible. Yet from this sparse environment, said Morse, "sprang an explosively curious mind." Standing in the bare-bones kitchen, I imagined Webster impatiently asking his mother to read another passage from the almanac (then spelled Johnson-style: *almanack*).[5] The local minister, Nathan Perkins, picked up on the boy's intellectual potential. Perkins became his tutor, visiting the Webster home to sit with Noah at the rectangular wooden table below the window opposite the hearth, working by candlelight on arithmetic, Latin, and Bible lessons. Completing the fable, Noah's father, despite financial strain, didn't resist Perkins's influence and eventually scraped together the money for his son's college tuition.

Noah graduated from Yale smack in the middle of the American Revolution. He earned a law degree, but began his career as a schoolteacher. Trying to teach children to read and write deepened his commitment to education and literacy, and inspired Webster to write a spelling book. He was only twenty-five when he wrote and published a thin volume known as *The Elementary Spelling Book* (originally bearing the title: *The First Part of the Grammatical Institute of the English Language*). The instruction book came to be known as the *Blue-Back Speller* because of its blue cover, and as the first of its kind in the New World, the *Speller* was a gargantuan success. With countless reprints and rip-offs over the next century, it would go on to sell upward of one hundred million copies.[6] Due to copyright woes, however, fortune eluded Webster, as if he'd been cursed by the ghost of Johannes Gutenberg. He had at least married well, at the age of thirty, to Rebecca Greenleaf, with whom he had eight children. But money was often a source of strain.

Webster wasn't a government official, but he elbowed his way to de facto statesman status through prolific writing, relationships with some of the Founding Fathers, and a knack for being in the right place at the right time, most notably the Constitutional Convention in Philadelphia in 1787. One of his essays was included among the eighty-five *Federalist Papers*, arguing for ratification of the Constitution.[7] He was a political animal, and in this sense he didn't think of his *Speller* as something that was merely about the lettering of words. It was in fact Phase 1 of his mission to help stitch the nascent nation together with words.

Across the country, statesmen fretted the lack of unity of the barely United States. Victory over the redcoats had neither unified the states, nor eliminated British cultural hegemony over its former colonies. Webster shared a fear with many people that the country might splinter at any moment, and he famously commented that the constituents of the nation were held together by nothing more than a cobweb. (It would take twentieth-century science to determine that spider silk is, pound for pound, one of the strongest substances on earth.)

The bold experiment of people ruling themselves, Webster believed, depended on a distinctly American language. Spread over vast terrain, the American people were speaking with varying accents and in a number of immigrant languages. Citizens needed to be speaking, if not with a single voice, at least in the same tongue. Common pronunciation and vocabulary throughout the land, Webster believed, would lead to a greater sense of kinship, which in turn would galvanize a spirit of shared culture and purpose. "Our political harmony," he wrote, "is therefore concerned in a uniformity of language." That uniformity was impossible without first removing "the clamor of pedantry" inherited from the English's English.[8] Whereas the British had used language to sustain class divisions, Webster, at least in principle, wanted it to bring people together.

A national language began with spelling. Webster was convinced that a streamlined and more consistent orthography would "demolish those odious distinctions of provincial dialects," making pronunciation the same from New York to Charleston. After purging the language of spelling ills inherited from the disowned mother country, the American language, he projected, would grow to become as distinct from Britain's English "as the modern Dutch, Danish, and Swedish are from the German, or from one another."[9] Call it nationalistic propaganda, a patriotic vision of an American identity, or language-obsessed sociological gibberish. Whatever it was, Webster believed the United States would at "some future time, be as distinguished by the superiority of her literary improvements, as she is already by the liberality of her civil and ecclesiastical constitutions."[10] "In his eyes," said Morse, "American language, literature, culture, spelling—all of this was all part of the same whole. The nation. If you had asked Webster whether the [survival of the] country depended on language or on democratic governance, he would have answered: 'Yes.'"

Webster was determined to be the founder of this new American tongue. But how to begin? He spent much of 1785 and 1786 road-tripping throughout the colonies, promoting his spelling book and lecturing about language. In Philadelphia, Benjamin Franklin attended one of his talks, and the two hit it off immediately. Franklin felt that the ever-widening gap between spelling and pronunciation was leading the language down a denigrating path toward a logographic orthography, in which symbols represent whole words, not a system for producing sound units, as in *c-a-t*. He considered languages like Mandarin ghastly for their memorization requirements, an "old manner of Writing" that was less sophisticated than a phonological alphabet. "If we go on as we have done a few Centuries longer," Franklin warned, "our words will gradually cease to express sounds, they will only stand for things." It was sound, he believed, that gave words their true power, and an optimal writing system must be based on a code for sounding out words.[11]

In his 1779 pamphlet, *A Scheme for a New Alphabet and Reformed Mode of Spelling*, Franklin tried to murder letters with notoriously variable pronunciation (*c*, *j*, *w*, *q*, *x*, and *y*). He also tried to use new ones for sounds represented by two letters, such as *sh*, as in *ship*, and *ng*, as in *spelling*. On top of that, he added new letter combinations, such as *ts* for the sound usually represented by "ch." (There are about forty-four sounds in most accents of spoken English, which means a phonetic alphabet with exactly one letter for one sound would have to have forty-four letters.) In the centuries to follow, other thinkers would also blame the alphabet for the twisted state of English written affairs. One of them was Mark Twain, who once said the English alphabet must have been "invented by a drunken thief."

At first, Webster disagreed with the senior statesman's ideas for changing the written word. As historian Jill Lepore explains: "Webster had mocked all proposals 'to alter the spelling of words, by expunging the superfluous letters.' He had wanted to standardize and Americanize spelling to get everyone speaking the same way, but he didn't think it wise to simplify the spelling code. Writing *favour* f-a-v-o-r seemed to him ridiculous." Although the language was full of spelling–pronunciation discord, Webster felt that trying to fix it would result in time wasted at best, and wholesale unintelligibility at worst.[12]

Yet as word meanings and pronunciations can change over time, so too did Webster's attitude about spelling reform. Perhaps, charmed by the renowned inventor-scholar-statesman and one-time printer, Webster was won over by Franklin's ideas and came to believe that major orthographic reform of some kind was "still practicable."[13] He began composing essays on the topic and sketching an orthography makeover of his own. "Strange as it may seem," he wrote in the preface to his first, much smaller dictionary in 1806, "the fact is undeniable that the present doctrin that no change must be made in writing words, is destroying the benefits of an alphabet, and reducing our language to the barbarism of Chinese characters instead of letters."[14]

Webster was in line with Franklin philosophically, but his prescription for the language was less radical, at least in terms of its visual impact: no new letters. What Webster did want, or believed necessary, was a streamlining and letter-swapping campaign across the lexicon. Letters like the *e* on the end of words such as *innovative, alternative, doctrine*, and *definite* had to go. So did the *a* in *bread*, the *u* in *armour*, the second *l* in *traveller*, and other "superfluous or silent letters." Webster also tried to remake words so that they contained more obvious signposts to pronunciation, which to his ear called for changing *grieve* to *greev, tongue* to *tung, women* to *wimmen, is* to *iz, sleigh* to *sley*, and *speak* to *speek*. And that was only the warm-up. *Thum, hed, bilt, fether, tuf, dawter*—Webster's ax(*e*) kept cutting.

Yet his suggested reforms gained little traction beyond Benjamin Franklin's reading room. Meanwhile, the *Speller*'s popularity hardly matched young Webster's vision of his own lofty destiny. Teaching hadn't gone well, his attempt at a magazine-writing career hadn't panned out, and, although he was eventually admitted to the

Connecticut bar, law wasn't putting wind in his sails or coinage in his pockets. If only he could make his views on spelling stick, history might remember him as the father of the American language.

What he overlooked, said Morse, is that "language can only be a unifying force if it's inclusive." Systematic change to orthography, no matter how reasonable, inevitably resembles commandments from on high. Americans may have already been culturally distinct from the British, but they shared the laissez-faire linguistic temperament that previously doomed efforts to form a language academy in London, and spelling reforms before that.[15] If anything, post–Revolutionary War Americans would have been even more resistant to an idea that smacked of the few telling the many how to behave.

Frustrated that an American tongue wasn't taking off, and possibly irritated by the lack of respect he felt he deserved from his Ivy League peers, Webster wrote the following in his journal on his thirtieth birthday: "30 years of my life gone! I have read much, written much, tried to do much good, but with little advantage to myself. I will now leave writing."[16] He had already written a bestseller used in classrooms throughout the country, and his *Sketches of American Policy*, published a few years before that thirtieth birthday, outlined a number of ideas about government that had worked their way into the Constitutional Convention and even into the Constitution. Yet Webster felt like a failure.

What he couldn't see was that he was accumulating the knowledge and experiences that he would later draw upon, first for the smaller *A Compendious Dictionary of the English Language* (1806), and then, much more so, for *An American Dictionary of the English Language* (1828). One such influence was his keen interest in the sciences. Illness was a less quarantined aspect to daily life back then, even though little was known about underlying biology. Webster read heavily on the subject, and later published two volumes on infectious disease. It's the kind of side interest illustrative of his information-devouring mind, and of his detective's instinct for getting to the bottom of things.

In 1800, Thomas Jefferson narrowly won the presidency and Federalists and Republicans clashed over how centralized the power of the nation should be. Many people, including Webster, thought the nation was on the brink of civil war, and the precarious state of the union renewed his conviction that a common language would be—must be—the nation's essential bonding agent.

Yet his belief in a national language wasn't purely altruistic in the "All men are created equal" sense of the word. In *A Is for America*, Lepore describes Webster as one in a series of white, upper-class, early Americans driven not by a noble duty to make English and education more accessible to the masses, but rather "to reform the language of those who already spoke it."[17] As many as 25 percent of the population of the US in 1790 didn't speak English as a first language. These people are conspicuously absent from Webster's writings about how to improve communication. His goal, it seems, was to eliminate pronunciation variation among American English speakers by making spelling more sensible. But what about the slaves, Native Americans, and immigrants who didn't speak English? Webster's reply might have been: "I'm sorry, who?"

Less honorable still, says Lepore, was the quest to circumvent language barriers through alphabet and/or language reform in the service of missionary practices that weren't exactly culturally sensitive. "You have to pay attention to who these reformers were," Lepore explained to me. "There are power issues historically, as far as how English was used to wipe out other languages. Suppression of sign language in the nineteenth century, for example—that's a harrowing story. What happened to indigenous languages—there's a very dark story there too." Webster, she said, is part of that legacy.

En route to West Hartford, I asked Morse about this issue because Lepore's point had unsettled my sense of Webster as a champion of the cause of the poor speller, nudging him closer to something along the lines of a bigoted crank. Morse's judgment is less condemning. "When you take modern sensibilities and apply them to those people back then, they're all schmucks and we shouldn't pay attention to them. To me, you want to try and get into their heads and imagine what they were attempting to do." In that sense, Webster wasn't out to persecute; he wanted, perhaps naïvely so, to revolutionize the language and save the Union, and he wasn't going to let the details of diversity stand in the way.

Webster joined the New York Philological Society, which was founded in 1788, for the "purpose of ascertaining and improving the American Tongue."[18] Yet by the turn of the millennium, he must have begun doubting whether hard-core spelling reform was a viable strategy for said ascertaining and improving. Instead of pushing an apparently unpopular idea, Webster shifted to a new tactic for defining this new language and its people, or at least the white English-speaking ones.

The Declaration of Independence was only a few decades old, but for more than a century, New World settlers had been developing vocabulary distinct from British English. This trend was in part a necessity; a panoply of new words for landscape features (*ponds* and *bluffs*[19]), animals (*skunks* and *rattlesnakes*), scientific principles (*nutrients* and *vaccines*), ideas of government (*caucuses* and *congressmen*), and foods (*chowder* and *succotash*) were sprouting up in and around the colonies. In addition, Native American words were being absorbed into the lexicon, words like *squash*, *terrapin*, *moose*, *moccasin*, *tomahawk*, and *opossum*, as were a continuous stream of new foreign words: *coleslaw* and *waffle* (Dutch), *bayou* and *butte* (French), *chocolate* and *tornado* (Spanish).[20] Webster heard this lexicographic expansion as evidence of an emerging language, and the need to inventory it in the pages of a dictionary.

Exactly when he anointed himself lexicographer of the land no one knows, but by 1800 Webster was soliciting advance orders for a "Dictionary of the American Language."[21] The idea was not well received. Johnson's *A Dictionary of the English Language*, by then forty-five years old and in its fifth edition, was still the gold standard—doubly so among Webster's fellow Federalists. These guys felt a political allegiance to the Crown and an even greater allegiance to British-ness. Johnson had carefully dressed the language up in a corset, and the Federalists didn't want to see it defiled. Some even suggested, as President John Adams did in 1780, that Congress establish a public institution—here we go again—"for refining, correcting, and ascertaining the English language."[22] (Johnson didn't exactly reciprocate the respect he received from across the Atlantic, calling Americans "Rascles-Robbers-Pirates . . . a race of convicts" that "ought to be thankful for anything we allow them short of hanging.")[23]

Yet Webster couldn't find much love for his idea among Republicans either. The plan for a dictionary, and nearly as often Webster himself, were skewered by the ruling members of both parties. One criticism of Webster's plan came from Joseph Dennie, a Boston-based journalist of Federalist persuasion: "If we once sanction the impertinence of individuals, who think themselves authorized to coin new words on every occasion, our language will soon become a confused jargon, which will require a new Dictionary every year."[24] Dennie's concern is strikingly familiar to that expressed by Englishman John Dryden 150 years earlier, who feared that an unmoored English would drift so far away from the English of history's literary greats that it would soon be unintelligible.

Stubborn, undeterred by naysayers, or both, Webster plowed ahead. In 1806 he published *A Compendious Dictionary of the English Language*. He was now a lexicographer first, spelling reformer second.[25] At 408 pages and containing 37,000 entries, the dictionary was modest by fat-book standards, yet impressive in that Webster completed it alone and in less than six years. Unlike Johnson's masterpiece, however, there were no quotations to enrich the short definitions—"orthoepy *noun*: the art of just pronunciation."[26] Still, the dictionary was audacious and controversial. For one thing, it included many new words; not just *pond* and *caucus* but also *appellate*, *gin* (cotton, not drink), *butternut*, *whiskey*, *chore*, *snowshoe*, and many more.

And new vocabulary was only the first part of his attempted language coup. Webster incorporated into the *Compendious Dictionary* what some people called "inventive spellings," but what Webster saw as orthographic repairs that any "man of taste" in his position would have made. It was nothing less than his duty to rid the lexicon of "palpable inconsistencies and preposterous anomalies" that dishonor English literature while perplexing students.[27] So *ploughed* became *plowed*, *almanack* became *almanac*, publick became *public*, *soup* became *soop*, *humour* became *humor*, determine became *determin*, *gaol* became *jail*, and *group* became *groop*.

The reception and sales of the 1806 dictionary were dismal. The original print run was seven thousand copies, and although the exact figures are unknown, it did not sell well; certainly not well enough to alleviate Webster's financial pressures.[28] A critic named James Savage chided Webster for believing that everyday people, not "learned men," could be "sovereigns over the realms of language."[29] It's an elegant summary of the more extreme prescriptivist worldview, if not an accidental admission that Savage and his ilk hadn't bothered to take to heart what Samuel Johnson had written about compiling his dictionary: "I have often been obliged to sacrifice uniformity to custom," Johnson wrote. Everyday usage rules.[30]

Here lies one of the most confounding aspects of Noah Webster's life and work. On the one hand, he produced firebrand Federalist writings and beliefs. As Lepore writes, he was part of a fraternity of "well-heeled men who loved England, hated France, favored strong central government and despised all that was common."[31] Webster certainly had the "hated France" thing down. In the preface to his 1806 dictionary, he explains the need for spelling reform by reflecting on Old and Middle English, and specifically how French and Latin influences "disfigured" the language "with a class of mongrels, *splendour, inferiour, authour,* and the like."[32] He blamed Johnson for his "reverence to usage" and unwillingness to weed out the "palpable absurdity" of the letter *u* in these and other words.

On the other hand, Webster demonstrated a distinctly populist, which is to say a (then) Republican philosophy toward English and the composition of the dictionary. "The man who undertakes to censure others for the use of certain words and to decide what is or is not correct in language seems to arrogate to himself a dictatorial authority, the legitimacy of which will always be denied."[33] Mixing spelling reform into this already muddied mindset only magnifies the impression of a contradictory set of opinions. How could the same man simultaneously hold descriptivist views of language, while expecting everyone to follow his prescribed orthographic wisdom? Equally conflicting is Webster's obsession with practical and efficient use of language and his understanding of how language evolves, versus his devotion to the impractical cause of spelling reform. Perhaps the best explanation for these apparent paradoxes is that in post-Revolutionary America, ideas about language were as variable as ideas about government. Webster, like the young nation itself, was struggling to find his identity.

Yet anyone who likes an underdog has got to admire Webster. In the wake of the failed first dictionary he readied himself for a lexicographical adventure that would dwarf his original effort.[34] In 1807, he began on the big kahuna, working within the doughnut hole of a circular desk in his home in New Haven. A few years later he moved with his family to Amherst, Massachusetts, where he continued to tirelessly weave definitions.

Webster originally thought the new dictionary would take five years, maybe a bit longer. It took twenty-five. When *An American Dictionary of the English Language* was published in 1828, America was a different country, and Webster a different man. As Lepore points out, opposition to the dictionary had vanished because the Federalist Party and most of Webster's enemies were dead. The rise of Republicanism, meanwhile, meant the egalitarian underpinnings of the dictionary, and the great wordsmith's descriptivist philosophy, were no longer incendiary. On the contrary, *An American Dictionary* was a welcome addition to nineteenth-century American homes. First-edition Johnson dictionaries were now more than seventy years old, and no less an authoritative figure than President Andrew Jackson was in need of this new reference book. Jackson was a crap speller.[35]

As he grew more mature, and as the years of defining went on, Webster either mollified his beliefs about spelling reform, or faked it for the sake of the dictionary's success and the financial security of his family. The smart money says he softened his once rebellious views. As historian Thomas Gustafson writes: "Webster's 1828 dictionary has been considered as much a work of cultural nationalism as his speller." But instead of being a linguistic Declaration of Independence, "the dictionary was the linguistic Treaty of Paris, wherein Webster maintains that while difference of language between England and America is inevitable, a sameness is desirable."[36] He had finally reconciled the language's—and the country's—relationship with Britain. The title change itself is telling. In his forties, when he set out to write a "Dictionary of the American Languagé," it was as if he was trying to strike a blow to the British (and Dr. Johnson) for their imperial grip on, well, everything. Two decades later, Webster realized that American English would never be as distinct from British English as Dutch is from German. English orthography would remain, for the most part, unchanged, and the title, *An American Dictionary of the English Language*, would do just fine.

The new dictionary cost about $20 ($364 today), which was about the same price as a grandfather clock.[37] It contained seventy thousand entries, compared to Johnson's forty-three thousand, although Webster did quite a lot of borrowing.* But with this new dictionary, Webster abandoned some of his early spelling reforms: *groop, speek, cloke, spunge, determin, bilt, fether, wimmen*. But he did manage to permanently alter, at least for American English, hundreds of other "outlaws of orthography."[38] *Jail* (gaol), *center* (centre), *theater* (theatre), *mask* (masque), *judgment* (judgement), *public* (publick), *music* (musick), *offense* (offence), *color* (colour), *mold* (mould), and more.

---

*Webster pulled generously from Johnson's dictionary. As H. L. Mencken put it, Webster was "sufficiently convinced of its merits to imitate it, even to the extent of lifting whole passages."

Expressions and occasional grammar rules separate American and British English today, but it's primarily differing spellings, most of them conceived by Webster, that compel publishers to print slightly different British and American editions of the same book.

The question of spelling evolution and revolution, Morse told me, is really a study of how people collectively reach consensus about the shape of words. "With Webster, the question is: Can one individual have an impact on that consensus?" Noah's life shows that the answer is, or at least it was, yes. His 1828 *American Dictionary of the English Language* wasn't a bestseller, primarily because of the price. But it was an immense achievement and is a landmark of American scholarship.

During our drive back to the Merriam-Webster offices in Springfield, Morse said there were many Noah Websters. The struggling schoolteacher, the later-in-life writer of acerbic essays, the idealistic youngster preaching about the ingredients of healthy democracy, the more tempered fifty-something, who replaced radical ideas for spelling reform with moderate and realistic goals. "Somewhere on that arc he's most interesting to me," said Morse. "When he sees that he can't be so idealistic, but he's not so bitter that he thinks improving society is impossible." It was a strange idea: that orthographic change could make the world a better place. But it was a catchy one, and would soon captivate some of the most powerful people in the world.

SEVEN

A FIRST CLASS MAN

We all work together for the great majoriti on which wi ar now agrid.[1]

Melvil Dewey

N THE SPRING OF 1902, Melvil Dewey readied himself for one of the most important dinners of his life.[2] He was to meet Andrew Carnegie, the steel magnate who, over the next decade, would become one of history's most celebrated philanthropists. During his lifetime, Carnegie bankrolled the construction of thousands of public libraries across the country, donating an estimated $350 million to promote literacy and learning (that's about $4.3 billion today).

In a letter to Carnegie leading up to the meeting, Dewey appealed to the businessman's interest in supporting what Carnegie called "a language commission." Juggling grandiosity and gumption, Dewey wrote:

I found 25 years ago the chief obstacle to getting the greatest good from public libraries was in the absurd spelling of English which ... wasted three years out of the school life of every English child who goes through a full course . . . [T]he greatest service that can be rendered the race today at a moderate cost is the endowment or at least the support for a few years of an office where a first class man with needed clerical assistance can answer questions and conduct a wise, conservative campaign for the simplification of English spelling.

If libraries were to really matter, reading needed to be easier. Dewey was certain that this language commission could make that happen: "In five years such an office would be so well started that its work might be turned over to the Carnegie Institution or to Columbia [University] or to some other prominent body. The best scholars of the world are agreed as to the need and as to its practicability."[3]

Born in 1851 to a Baptist family in upstate New York, Dewey was educated in his hometown of Adams Center, not far from the eastern shores of Lake Ontario, before heading to Amherst College. He was a keen student and compulsive diary keeper. From the age of fifteen he recorded in spreadsheet format his age, height, weight, and financial assets. When he was seventeen, he was caught in a fire at school. Dewey scrambled out of the building carrying a stack of books. He had inhaled such a dangerous amount of smoke that, when he subsequently came down with a cough, a local doctor said he would not survive. But Dewey recovered, and as he did he became that much more determined to never waste time, and to devote his days to a life mission of promoting "a higher education for the masses."[4]

He was just a few years out of college, working as an assistant librarian, when he devised the classification scheme for library books that would come to be known as the Dewey Decimal System. In his later years, he recalled its genesis: Listening to a church sermon, all at once "the solution flasht over me so that I jumpt in my seat and came very near shouting 'Eureka!' Use *decimals* to number a classification of all human knowledge in print."[5]

Before meeting Carnegie, Dewey, who would spend more than fifty years of his life struggling on behalf of spelling reform, must have felt immense pressure to make a convincing case. He finally had the ear of the one man who not only held similar convictions about education, but who also had unprecedented power to effect widespread change. The librarian obsessed over how to make his pitch so as "not to scare our capitalist," as he confided to a friend. "He is a peculiar man . . . " and "a hard trout to get on your hook."[6]

Soon after the turn of the century, Carnegie had turned his full energies to philanthropy. When the two men met for dinner, Carnegie was, if not actively shopping for a new cause to support, at least willing to hear yet another plug for funding. The Spelling Reform Association (later called the Simplified Spelling Board), which Dewey had helped establish in 1876, was building an ever-more distinguished list of supporters: legislators, educators, artists, newspaper editors, publishers, university presidents, and scholars throughout the "cuntry" and in Canada and Britain. But funding was a perpetual problem.

There are no minutes from their initial dinner, and it would be a couple of years before Carnegie would open his checkbook. But by Dewey's account, he had played a good hand. Writing to a colleague afterward, he reported using "all the skill and finesse possible to avoid hunting wild ducks with a brass band." Carnegie, he added, "is more interested and more enthusiastic than ever. He says unqualifiedly that no cause he has ever helpt appeals to him so strongly." Carnegie was in.[7]

* * *

IN THE DECADES following publication of Webster's 1828 dictionary, orthography debate fell into a relatively quiet period. Perhaps Webster's great work was so comprehensive that people felt the language had reached a level of clarity and stability whereby it no longer needed refinement. If a source as authoritative as the dictionary accepted so many irregular spellings, maybe it was best to leave them be. Besides, there were other matters requiring attention, like Manifest Destiny and the debate over slavery that was steadily dividing the nation in two. Johnson's dictionary had helped settle English orthography, Webster gave it some American spice, and, for the most part, the way words were spelled was a done deal.

But not everyone had come to terms with English spelling. In 1844, Bartłomiej Beniowski, a Polish ex-pat living in London, self-published "the Anti-Absurd Alphabet." In one sense, Beniowski's "phrenotypic alphabet" is just one in a long string of orthographies devised by eccentrics possessing unusual patience and a particular compulsion for ordering things that strike them as disorderly. What makes Beniowski's plan stick out, however, is its tantrum tenor. He allocates more than half of the entire volume to rant about "tyrannically ridiculous nonsense," "nonsensical ridiculosities," and "INCUBUS-LIKE ABSURDITIES" of the English alphabet (his caps), and to lambaste the "chicken-headed" people who defend it. The ridiculosities include the fact that *a* "represents four sounds as different from one another as black from white, yellow, or green; witness *a*pe, *a*rm, *a*pple, *a*ll," and that *f* "is called *ef*, but, in the word *'of '* which meets the eye at every moment of our existence, *f* is to be pronounced *v*; thus write *of*, read *ov*. Besides, the sound *f* is also represented by *gh*, as in *laugh*."[8]

But buried in Beniowski's tirade is something strangely hopeful. He was "convinced that the freedom of the human race may be achieved by the powers at the disposal of the present English generation." This is a remarkable statement in a book that devotes so much ink to celebrating the languages of Hebrew, Greek, Latin, Russian, and Polish, while slamming English and its users. But Beniowski also revered the English way of life and government, which made it that much more frustrating to him that the nation's power to spread freedom remained paralyzed, "reduced to nothing, by the ignorance of the masses" that had been ensured by the pitiful spelling code. "Britons," he screamed, "alter your alphabet—alter your orthography—make your language easy—speak to the world—be intelligible—and you shall conquer and liberate nations . . . " Somehow, Beniowski failed to see any connection between the individual freedoms that were cornerstones of the system of government he so respected, and the unpoliced use of language.

The reforms required to rescue English, writes Beniowski, should be well known by now to anyone who has ever thought for a minute about language. "Return to the Hebrew alphabet," "reject the double final consonants," and decide on one letter to represent one sound only, even if that means instituting new letters, and stick to that agreement "without any exceptions, restrictions, or provisos." Scholars adhering to the prescription of "Anti-absurdities" will, after a mere six months, look back on spellings of old and have "an unavoidable, insuperable, supernatural difficulty" abstaining from "laughing at the shocking orthography of the present writers."[9]

On the other side of the ocean, at the foot of the Wasatch Mountains and facing a vast salt lake, a religious leader was trying not only to clean up the confounding spelling system, but also to reinvent the alphabet. Brigham Young, president of the Latter Day Saints Church, was pulled into the world of spelling reform by a thirty-nine-year-old Englishman named George D. Watt.[10] In the 1830s, Watt learned a shorthand system developed by a teacher back in England, which sparked in him a wider interest in alternative writing schemes. When he migrated to America five years later, Mormonism's first British convert brought with him some unconventional ideas about spelling.

In the 1850s, Watt and other Church higher-ups were developing a school system and, with Young's endorsement, devised a thirty-eight-character alphabet. The best part: Not one of the letters from the standard English system was used. It was called the Deseret Alphabet, and over the next decade classes were taught to promote the new code, type was made for printing, ten thousand dollars was allocated for new textbooks, and the groovy new characters even adorned Mormon coins.[11] And just so there's no confusion on this point: The Deseret Alphabet is not the mysterious code written by God on the gold plates that Joseph Smith, founder of Mormonism, unearthed on a hill in Manchester, New York in 1827. Watt's alphabet, in contrast, was merely a new way to write words to God.

Like Beniowski and other reformers, the Mormons justified the scheme by pointing to the difficulties of the English spelling system and how, in Young's words, "the years that are now required to learn to read and spell can be devoted to other studies."[12] Yet unlike language mavericks past, the Mormons saw the new system as a way to both include and exclude. Newcomers to the land (and faith) would more quickly assimilate into the culture if they had a more efficient alphabet and spelling system by which to learn the language. At the same time, an orthography of their own would give the Mormons a linguistic bunker, protecting them from outside forces that looked unfavorably on the newcomer religion.[13]

The Deseret alphabet didn't take and, tirades like Beniowski's notwithstanding, the mid-nineteenth century saw a lull in efforts to remake the alphabet or reform English spelling. In contrast, this same period marks a burst of creativity in the area of constructed languages: languages made from scratch for the idealistic purpose of universal comprehension. Chief among these were the languages of Volapük, Esperanto (with its later spinoff, Ido), and then, in 1903, one called Latino Sine Flexione.

Volapük came first, designed between 1879 and 1880 by a Roman Catholic priest in Germany named Johann Martin Schleyer. Like many before him, Schleyer's religious convictions motivated him to dive into linguistic innovation. Appearing to the priest in a dream, God told him to develop an international language. "Go forth and fix the words so as to better spread My word," or something along those lines. But Volapük was soon eclipsed by a simpler tongue endowed with a more enchanting name.

Esperanto is "The International Language That Works!" according to its Web site, where banners also declare that it's "A Second-Language for Everyone" and "A Gateway to the World." Esperanto is alive and well today, or at least alive. Designed in 1887 by Dr. L. L. Zamenhof, the son of Lithuanian Jews living in the Polish town of Białystok, Esperanto was developed for that same simple magnificent goal: Reverse the curse of Babel. In the Book of Genesis, God is none too pleased with the residents of the peaceful and cosmopolitan city of Babylon. They had set their sights on building a tower that would reach the heavens, and were getting along so well that they almost pulled it off. To cut their effort short, end the harmonious coexistence of diverse peoples, or both, God confused their tongues, thereby introducing humanity to the concept, "lost in translation."

Zamenhof, an ophthalmologist (no wonder he didn't like English spellings) and philologist, called himself "Dr. Esperanto"—one who hopes. Esperanto is essentially a goulash tongue consisting of romance language vocabulary and Slavic sound units. Some two million people worldwide allegedly speak Esperanto, although I'm skeptical as to how many are fluent speakers versus those who dabble for the sake of an oddball party trick, like chiming in with a little Klingon (from *Star Trek*) or J. R. R. Tolkien's Elvish. Creators of Esperanto and other constructed languages aimed to have easy-to-learn grammars and avoid spelling irregularities by using more phonetic orthographies. But they have always had a host of marketing and sticking-power problems. *Ili neniam sumi is pli ol kurioza oj*, which is Esperanto for: They never really amounted to much more than curiosities.[14]

But what did get off the ground in the mid-nineteenth century was the most ambitious and authoritative English-language undertaking in history: compilation of the *Oxford English Dictionary*. Launched in 1857, the project would take twenty-seven years before the first portion was published, as James Murray and his team meticulously hunted etymologies and gathered together words and definitions mailed in by volunteers from across Britain, including the "madman," W. C. Minor, a patient in residence at the Broadmoor Criminal Lunatic Asylum.

Somehow, spelling got hot again. What triggered the resurgence is difficult to say. The steady march of science and reason, sparked in part by Darwin's *Origin of Species* (1859), may have been a factor, insofar as people were thinking about the processes of gradual change over time. Reading was a mighty engine, as Dewey once put it, but to science- and engineering-inclined people of the late nineteenth century, English was beginning to look more and more like a machine in need of repair.

By 1877, orthography enthusiasts in London were circulating a petition for a Spelling Reform Conference, led by the eminent Oxford professor of Sanskrit and Comparative Philology, Max Müller. The flyer called for action on a matter of "growing national misfortune." "Language is not made for scholars and etymologists," railed Müller, "and if the whole race of English etymologists were really swept away by the introduction of Spelling Reform, I hope they would be the first to rejoice in so good a cause." Uniting with their American brothers, the British reformers pointed to legislative action in Connecticut and Massachusetts as evidence (albeit somewhat inflated evidence—these were only "committees to consider the feasibility . . . ") that the Americans were moving ahead with reforms to help address the problem of 5.5 million "illiterate persons" in the US.

Equally alarming to the new reformers was the fact that promotion of English "in Japan, China, and the Islands of the Pacific was greatly hindered by the same cause." For traders and evangelicals alike, the spelling code hurt business. A simplified orthography was the key to turning the world into what Dewey called the "English speaking race." It was Webster's nation binding on a global scale with a Christian spin, brought to you by Babel v2.0.

DEWEY'S GIVEN NAME was Melville, but as a teenager he started writing it *Melvil*. On his twenty-eighth birthday, he changed his last name to "Dui."[15] The name stuck, for a while, until he applied for a job at Columbia University. He was hired as "Librarian-in-

Chief," on condition that he jettison, or at least be subtler about, his unorthodox views regarding orthography and use the original spelling of his family name.[16] Although a future Columbia president would become a knight of Dewey's round table of spelling reformers, at the time Dewey was applying for the job, University officials wanted nothing to do with the renegade spelling movement. (Soon after he was hired, the librarian formerly known as Dui received a letter from a friend: "I am very glad to see that you write your name *Dewey*. Now pray lay aside some, at least, of your orthographical peculiarities, and spell like common folk.")

Dewey was a frighteningly organized human being. His journals, usually written in shorthand, reveal an obsession with streamlining and efficiency. For a period of years, he and his wife Annie would start off every month by composing a to-do list. Her categories included: "Exercise 1 hr; Self-Culture, 1 hr; Sing 15 Min; Don't waste a minute." His to-dos were things like, "Horse-back 3 a week; Dress *well*; Short, organized letters; Rise early; eat slowly; Make no promises; Breathe deeply, sing, and settle cash daily."[17] Such was the temperament of the man who chose as his three primary pursuits in life, library organization, simplification of English spelling, and promotion of the metric system.

When the American Philological Society launched in 1876, its members determined to use and promote a dozen new spellings. They were: *tho, altho, thru, thruout, thoro, thoroly, thorofare, program, prolog, catalog, pedagog,* and *decalog.* That same year, Dewey, then only twenty-five, attended the International Convention for the Amendment of English Orthography in Philadelphia, where he hobnobbed with a community of learned men committed to "the good cause." Out of that convention sprang the Spelling Reform

Association, with Dewey as its secretary on paper, and pied piper in practice. By the end of the decade, his optimism was iridescent. "A few years ago," he wrote, "it required some hardihood for an educated man to declare himself in favor of simplified spelling, but since the founding of the Spelling Reform Association in 1876 every prominent student of English living, both American and foreign, has conceded that scholarship, as well as common sense, requires the change which is quietly but steadily going forward."

Spelling reform was gaining traction. In 1894, Senator W. E. Chandler of New Hampshire introduced to Congress a resolution: "To encourage better spelling of the English language, to make easier, more logical, and more rapid the world of pupils in learning to read, and to reduce the cost of printing and writing." The bill called upon the country's Public Printer to begin printing all government materials with words spelled according to rules developed by the Philological Society of England and the American Philologic Society, to wit: *rough* becomes *ruf*; *written* becomes *writin*; *cider* becomes *sider*; and *parliament* becomes *parlament*.[18] The resolution failed but similar government action was on the horizon, this time from the White House.

Dewey was assiduously building support for the Spelling Reform Association. The president of Oberlin College, a member of the Board of Regents for the University of Arizona, and a professor at the University of Texas all wrote in to give him the thumbs-up, as did a correspondent from the *Boston Times*, who suggested that he and Dewey team up to publish a weekly newspaper printed with simplified spelling. Little old ladies in Alabama; newspaper editors from New York to Wyoming; a St. Louis printer who had published a phonetic edition of The Gospel of Matthew; the Illinois State Teachers'

Association, a Boston shoemaker, and the publishing company of Funk & Wagnall's, the owners of which wrote Dewey in 1890 to say how much they "heartily believe[d] in the movement," and wanted to publish a dictionary that would meet Dewey's approval.[19]

One such letter of support was from the Education Office of Nova Scotia, dated June 12, 1896. Channeling the spirit of Benjamin Franklin, Mr. A. H. Mackay warns Dewey of anticipated disapproval from literary types, who are "undoubtedly afflicted with that conservatism so characteristic of the unscientific literary hack . . . Our literary men have a tendency to become fossilized as they are in China . . . And if you allow the United States to be controlled by them alone, in a generation or two you will be as conservative as the Celestial kingdom itself."[20]

By the time Benjamin Ide Wheeler delivered his the 1906 commencement address to Stanford's Calamity Class, Dewey's good cause had operatives on the faculties of Yale (five), Stanford, Harvard, Columbia, MIT, Bucknell, Reed College, Whitman College, Western Reserve, Lafayette College, the Alabama Girls' Technical Institute, and Jefferson Medical College—to name a handful. "And why have these men suggested and effected changes in the language?" asked John Earle Uhler, a professor of English at Louisiana State University and chairman of the local Simplified Spelling Leag. "For the very same reason that engineers rear levees along a river, dig new channels, dam old outlets—to make the river serve man, not control him." The public urgently needed to be led out of this "orthografic swamp."

But what did Dewey actually do as leader of this rebellion? During meetings, Board members would sometimes debate various schemes or word revisions. Other times, they drifted off topic, discussing Shakespeare's *Othello* one month, politics the next.* When proceedings were steered back to the subject of spelling reform, Dewey would chime in about specific word alterations, but he worried about putting the cart before the horse. He knew that in the eyes of the public, spelling reform treaded precariously close to navel gazing for the rich. Until the movement could garner wider support, he felt that combating this credibility shortage was of paramount concern, and that nitpicking among themselves over a certain vowel inflection or problems caused by the *c* in *backing* and *lacking* would not move things forward. So Dewey focused instead on generating political momentum.

The whiff of realism in his approach may appear at odds with the pie-in-the-sky nature of Dewey's chosen crusade. But dismissing his aims as quixotic belies his previous accomplishment, as well as the lasting legacies of individuals like Johnson and Webster. If they could wrestle the language into the pages of a dictionary, and if Dewey himself could create a system for organizing all "human knowledge in print," why should he have thought that tackling the spelling system was in any way out of reach?

To prevent the movement from appearing fringe, Dewey drew upon the same compulsive-guy resources that made him a champion to-do-list maker and diary keeper, and built a coalition. He wrote, collected, and organized, then wrote, collected, and organized some more, corresponded with members and potential members, and authored umpteen commentaries and letters to editors in

---

*During one meeting, Harvard philology professor and Dante expert, Charles Hall Grandgent, who referred to himself as a "frothy anarchist," proclaimed that "no Harvard student ever misspells a word." (Dewey Archive, Box 86, pp. 42 and 55 of 1912 SSB meeting minutes)

a nonstop effort to attract publicity. In an 1891 note to the editor of the *Albany Times*, he waxed on about whether *employee* should have the second *e* on the end.[21] In another letter, he complains to a dictionary publisher about adverb formations—*academically* from *academic*, or *geologically* from *geologic*, which he felt were ill-conceived constructions, and that the words could stand on their own without the *ly*. "Is there any authority for it, or any serious authority against it?"[22] He was trying to bludgeon his fellow countrymen into changing their habits of language, one exhaustive communiqué at a time. (The reply to his note about adverbs wasn't warm: "There is the best authority for it," wrote a Mr. Charles Scott, "namely the law of the English language, which allows the formation of an adverb in 'ly' from any adjective whatever. The authority of next greatest weight, the fact of current use, of the given form, happens, by various slight accidents of history which I could state at length if necessary, not to exist for most words of this kind.")

Dewey could lock horns over minutiae one minute, yet in the next speak of "gradual" reform— "a wise, conservative campaign." No Benjamin Franklin–styled alphabectomy, and no wholesale re-write of the lexicon. Change would be delicate and incremental, bordering on undetectable. This practical view of what could and could not be achieved, and how fast, shaped Dewey's philosophy throughout a life of armchair activism.[23] That didn't mean the orthography of his efficiency-obsessed dreams wasn't substantially different looking from the spelling of his time.* But Dewey knew the

---

*To the converted, he had no problem penning sentences like this one, from June of 1914: "There ar so fu ov us that ar foloin this thin up thoroli that we must kip in close tuch." How Dewey couldn't see the confusion caused by foloin and sirloin, as in steak, is beyond me. (Dewey Archive, Box 39, June 19 letter to Mr. N. J. Werner)

reform movement's legitimacy depended on a cautious pace, and he incessantly tried to distinguish his campaign from what he saw as wacky and unresearched proposals put forth by overeager "cranks and extremists who have made the cause look ridiculous."[24]

By the look of the extensive collection of spelling-related postcards, letters, newspaper clippings, and other materials piled into the Melvil Dewey Papers at Columbia, one might conclude that he was a pathological hoarder. With all that paper, he built in his mind a fortress, shielding him from scorn and ridicule. The hundreds of names he had gathered in support of the cause were a far cry from comprising a critical mass. Yet by surrounding himself with the hard-copy weight of encouragement from people across the continent, some of whom really did carry legitimate influence, Dewey hypnotized himself into thinking the movement was chugging along.

ANDREW CARNEGIE ENDOWED the Simplified Spelling Board to the tune of about twenty-five thousand dollars a year for the decade beginning in 1906.[25] In what appears to have been just that initial dinner with Dewey and a few follow-up meetings, the librarian-metric-system-enthusiast-spelling-reform advocate had talked the tycoon out of parting with an impressive sum. Of course, from Dewey's perspective, Carnegie's backing was no lucky strike. It was another step toward the inevitable new orthography. The details of the new spelling system were beside the point; the current one was a mess, everybody knew it, and with enough political and public support, a better one could be crafted and strategically implemented.

During his first year or two supporting the Simplified Spelling Board, Carnegie most likely wanted to see what this "language commission" could accomplish. In the vernacular of today's venture philanthropy, his donations were seed money. That he went well beyond just a year or two of support reveals Carnegie's commitment to the cause and his trust of, and patience with, Dewey's plodding campaign.

Carnegie's endorsement and dollars were a huge boost for the members of the Board. Spelling reform had now reached the upper echelons of academia and the private sector, and it was about to do the same in government. In August 1906, President Theodore Roosevelt ordered the federal printing office to use three hundred novel spellings, as prescribed by the Simplified Spelling Board. *Dasht* (from *dashed*), *deposit* (from *deposite*), *good-by* (from *good-bye*, not *goodbye*), *instil* (from *instill*), *prest* (from *pressed*), *surprize* (from *surprise*), *thorofare* (from *thoroughfare*), and *vizor* (from *visor*). A few months earlier, Roosevelt had written Columbia professor and Board member, James Brander Matthews, to let him know that the president's personal secretary, William Loeb, "himself an advanced spelling reformer, will hereafter see that the President, in his correspondence, spells the way you say he ought to!"[26]

Roosevelt himself wasn't much of a speller, and the arguments set forth by Dewey and his crew resonated with the president's idea of common sense. Advocates of orthographic reform had pointed out, rather shrewdly, that qualified applicants to the federal office of the Civil Service Commission had been rejected because of spelling errors. Roosevelt had served in the Commission, and the Simplifiers may have been playing to his interests.[27] Roosevelt also fraternized with some of the key players, including Matthews, whom he had invited to the White House, and Carnegie, who had once called Roosevelt a "prince in the republic of letters."*28

After the presidential edict, the Associated Press reported on August 28 that "an official list of the 300 reformed words reached the executive office yesterday," and that "a meeting called by Public Printer [Charles] Stillings, of all the chief clerks of the various departments, and a committee was appointed to formulate rules for carrying out this order."29 The president's letter to Stillings enclosed the circular published by the Simplified Spelling Board, more copies of which, Roosevelt informed Stillings, "can be obtained free from the Board at No. 1 Madison Avenue, New York City."30 Dewey, back in the office with his typewriter and stacks of flyers, must have been doing cartwheels.

Roosevelt didn't think the spelling measure was "anything very great at all." He saw it as a modest and logical first step toward making "our spelling a little less foolish and fantastic."31 Just as *fysshe* and *publick* were now archaic constructions, so too should *night* and *thorough* be turned into *nite* and *thoro*. "There is not the slightest intention to do anything revolutionary or initiate any far-reaching policy," Roosevelt said. Many of the three hundred spellings were already part of everyday usage. Today about half of them are (for example, *catalog*, *caliber*, *gelatin*, and *rancor*, formerly *catalogue*, *calibre*, *gelatine*, and *rancour*), but these changes were organic. "The purpose is simply for the Government, instead of lagging behind

---

*Roosevelt may have been exposed to the idea of updating English orthography much earlier in his life. As a student at Harvard in the 1880s, he had a class with the famed psychologist and philosopher, William James. Well before the heyday of the Simplified Spelling Board, James had written to a friend, "Isn't it abominable that everybody is expected to spell the same way? Let us get a dozen influential persons, each to spell after his own fashion and so break up this tyranny."

popular sentiment, to advocate abreast of it and at the same time abreast of the views of the ablest and most practical educators of our time as well as the most profound scholars."

The press had an absolute field day with the president's order. The *New York Times* vowed to correct Roosevelt's "freak" spellings as if they were typos. The *Baltimore Sun* asked if the president would now spell his name *Rusevelt*, or whether he'd "get down to the fact and spell it 'butt-in-sky.'" The *Evening Post* presciently stated: "This is 2 mutch."[32] A century later, President George W. Bush was hit with a similar barrage for gaffes—sorry, alternative pronunciations— like *subliminimal* and *nucular*, but at least Bush wasn't ordering all members of the executive branch to adopt his unusual pronunciations. (*Nucular*, by the way, was added to the *OED* in 2003.)

But the British press made the American media response look friendly by comparison. An August 25, 1906, article tagged as a "Special Cable to the *New York Sun* and *Buffalo Courier*," reported that the London newspapers were calling Roosevelt an anarchist. "They do not go quite so far as to suggest lynching, yet it is clear that some of the leaders [headlines] in the evening papers were written while steam poured from the collars of the enraged editors." Editors at the *Evening Standard* wrote: "[H]ow dare this Roosevelt fellow . . . dictate to us how to spell a language which is ours while America is still a savage and undiscovered country . . . Our language is our own and we shall write it as is proper." Other articles railed against "barbarisms" like *thru* and called the president's action "Yanky Panky." The *Globe* posited that Roosevelt, like William the Conqueror, will find "it is easier to subdue a people than a language." After conceding that Walt Whitman wrote something that could fairly be called poetry, The *Globe* editors pointed out "that in literature the United States still remains a province of England."[33] Mr. President, get your damn hands off our language.

Members of the other branches of government were likewise less than pleased with the commander in chief. Despite the fact that Supreme Court Justice David J. Brewer was a member of the Simplified Spelling Board, the high court ignored the new spellings as they applied to any of its publications.[34] When Congress returned to session after the summer break, opposition was swift. The House ordered an inquiry into the president's action, and passed a resolution directing the public printer to ignore Roosevelt's three hundred spellings and "observe and adhere to the standard of orthography prescribed in generally accepted dictionaries of the English language."[35] In December, when it seemed that the president's orthography was headed for debate on the Senate floor, where it, and Roosevelt, would surely be burned, the president rescinded the order. One December 13 newspaper headline read: "Old-Fashioned Words Are to Prevail."

Historians and biographers have, understandably, dismissed Roosevelt's foray into spelling reform as a wacky pet project. Yet in light of the firestorm of opposition from London and accusations at home of czarlike tendencies, the printing order may have hurt Roosevelt's reputation more than you might think. "President Roosevelt's spelling order has done him more harm than perhaps any other act of his since he became President," wrote a *New York Times* correspondent in London.[36] The episode was a humorous one, yes. But it prompted more than lighthearted editorials. After all, this was a president who would famously say: "I don't think that any harm comes from the concentration of powers in one man's hands." Congress viewed the spelling edict as an example of precisely this kind of "energetic use of the executive power."[37] The speed at which the public and other branches of government moved to rein him in and reassert the constitutionally designated boundaries of his, and indeed the US government's, authority, further illustrated just how upset people were.

To his credit, Roosevelt was at least aware of his habit of stepping over the line. " . . . [A] President," he wrote to a friend in 1907, "ought not to go into anything outside of his work as President. But it is rather a hard proposition to live up to."[38] Then again, his international reputation couldn't have been too tarnished. A few months later, Roosevelt became the first American to win the Nobel Peace Prize, for his role in brokering an end to the Russo-Japanese War.

"IT IS HARD to say which is more remarkable," writes author Bill Bryson, "the number of influential people who became interested in spelling reform or the little effect they had on it." At no time in history is this observation more salient than during the early years of the twentieth century, and especially during the Roosevelt administration. If Dewey's office on Madison Avenue wasn't outright buzzing, it was certainly more active than it ever had been or would be again. The president, a Supreme Court justice, the United States Commissioner of Education, Mark Twain, a group called the National Education Association,[39] *OED* founding editor Murray, dozens of top academics, institutions, printers, and journalists, and Andrew Carnegie were all on board. Simplified spelling was threatening to be the next big thing. So what went wrong?

The first answer is the one that jumps to mind for many people when they first hear about spelling reform: It's unrealistic. I'm not talking about a three hundred–word list of tweaked words, half of which are spellings that have naturally been making their way into regular use. I'm talking about simplified spelling in the thousands-of-words sense, the way people like Hart, Webster (initially), and Dewey envisioned. It's unrealistic because of the inevitable confusion it would trigger; the impracticality of remaking the alphabet, if that's your chosen tactic; the impossibility of recasting English words to read phonetically no matter the accent; the costs of changing printing infrastructure; the hazard of a comprehension gap between present and past orthography; and the perpetual infighting among the revolutionaries themselves as to the nuts and bolts of reform. "There's just no easy fix," Crystal once told me. "Not for a spelling system that was six hundred years in the making."

In a strange twist, the reform effort may also have been hurt by the endorsement of such prominent figures. John Gable, executive director of the Theodore Roosevelt Association, speculates that Roosevelt's connection with spelling reform was actually counterproductive to the cause. "All of a sudden it became about Roosevelt and his egotism—that he could think he could rewrite the English language." Roosevelt was such an irresistible target for ridicule through cartoons and editorials, that spelling reform became "a laughing stock in a way it might not have been."[40] The writer H. L. Mencken noted that "the buffoonery characteristically thrown about the matter by Roosevelt, served only to raise up enemies."[41] In a similar vein, the very nature of public interest in, and scrutiny of, rich and powerful people made Carnegie's association with spelling reform suspicious, as if the innocuous subject of orthography was linked to some shady corporate agenda.[42]

Another setback was the decision to hold the annual Board meetings at New York's prestigious Waldorf-Astoria hotel. Dewey and company constantly struggled to gain credibility and deflect accusations that spelling reform was little more than a frivolous form of gentlemen's recreation. It's perplexing, then, that the Board paid for members from out of town to stay at the Waldorf, with their families, and hosted a lavish banquet with custom-made menus.

That's not to say the meetings were all truffles and trifles. On the agenda for the 1913 gathering were a selection of papers including: "The Use of S and Z for their Respectiv Sounds in all Cases," presented by Professor Oliver F. Emerson of Western Reserve, and "Simplification of Spelling in Ancient Times, or the Origin of the Greek Alfabet," presented by Professor George Hempl of Stanford. But by and large the Waldorf meetings epitomized a campaign that, in the eyes of more and more people, was a waste of time and energy.

Still, imagine what might have happened if Carnegie, so taken with spelling reform, had augmented his commitment to the tune of a few more zeros. He had signed on, after all, because he believed in education—the same reason that led him to the cause of public libraries. It's not outlandish to think that a certain action here or conversation there might have led the brash capitalist to conclude that a changed spelling system was the key to literacy and education.

In 1917, Carnegie gave his final donation to the Board, soon after which he decided that the group was "useless." "I think I have been patient long enuf," he wrote. "I have much better use for twenty-five thousand dollars a year."[43] That's not to say that he abandoned the idea at heart. When World War I began in 1914, after most of his contemporaries had already severed their connection to simplified spelling, Carnegie wondered aloud whether an improved English orthography would have catalyzed enough international understanding to have prevented the Great War.[44] Dewey wrote one of Carnegie's handlers in 1917, about the philanthropist's decision to turn off the faucet: "The war makes it dubly desirabl to work just now. Mr Carnegie's great interest was becauz he saw that this wud help imensly in making English the world language, and war conditions are paving the way for this as never befor. In the language of the prayerbook, I beg and beseech yu not to make this dredful mistake."[45]

Over the next two decades, the movement slowed to a barely perceptible crawl. Dewey, refusing to let the flame burn out, kept at it with his writing and occasional publicity, and the topic received a bit of attention now and then, whenever a public figure felt like lamenting the challenging inconsistencies of English spelling. George Orwell called the spelling code "preposterous." H. L. Mencken famously wrote: "'Correct spelling,' indeed, is one of the arts that are far more esteemed by schoolma'ams than by practical men, neck deep in the heat and agony of the world." John Steinbeck was sloppy with spelling (*freindship* was one of his frequent slips) and worse with punctuation. His wife, Carol, copyedited and retyped most of his work. Corresponding with a friend and aspiring writer in 1929, Steinbeck wrote: "I want to speak particularly of your theory of clean manuscripts, and spelling as correct as a collegiate stenographer, and every nasty little comma in its place and preening of itself. 'Manners,' you say it is, and knowing the 'trade' and the 'Printed Word.' But . . . I have the instincts of a minstrel rather than those of a scrivener," he said, preferring to leave to copy editors the work of comma patrol and spelling "so that school teachers will not raise their eyebrows."[46]

In 1934, the *Chicago Tribune* published an item mentioning that its editor and publisher, Colonel Robert R. McCormick, was changing the spelling of his name to *M'Cormick*. It was probably a joke, but McCormick wasn't kidding when he made it house style for the paper to use a short list of simplified spellings, including *frate* (*freight*), *cigaret* (*cigarette*), and *nite* (*night*).[47] He insisted on these spellings for decades, but to little or no effect beyond his newspaper.

By the 1940s, academics were still talking about the "defect" of present-day English spelling and likening irregularly spelled words to "picture languages."[48] But by then few people had anything much to say, with the notable and enraged exception of playwright George Bernard Shaw. Shaw called for a new alphabet and new orthography to "prescribe an official pronunciation," and he left a little money in his will as a cash prize for someone who could come up with a new English alphabet.[49] Like Dewey, Shaw was consumed by the idea that people, especially children, were wasting time learning a "foolish orthography based on the notion that the business of spelling is to represent the origin and history of a word instead of its sound and meaning."[50]

Toward the end of his life, Dewey didn't so much give in as retreat. He spent more and more time at the Lake Placid Club in the Adirondacks, where, as acting president of the Club, he managed to maintain his bubble of altered orthography. One 1922 Club "Brekfast" menu featured *sausaj, cofi,* and *huni gridl cakes with Vermont maple sirup.* A few weeks before his death in December of 1931, Dewey wrote a letter "to a fu personal frends" reporting good health. He was now eighty years old. "So whyl the world has more to wori about than ever befor in human histori I am bizi & hapi not becauz I am indifferent to thez present problems but becauz my mind is skoold not to wori." The Simplified Spelling Board was dead. But by then, the torch had already been passed.

Years earlier, while international attention focused on orthography fireworks in the US, another cadre of dissidents was regrouping in England. On September 10, 1908, ten scholars met in the York Room of London's Holborn Restaurant. Among them were two members of the Simplified Spelling Board. The Americans had come to debrief their fellow reformers about strategies that were and weren't working back in the US. That night, the Englishmen established a satellite group that they called the Simplified Spelling Society.

They lay low, sometimes dormant, for nearly a century. But they did not die out, as if awaiting just the right time and place to re-emerge. They may have found it in modern-day Washington DC. Every spring since 2004, a handful of them have gathered in the nation's capital to picket outside the Scripps National Spelling Bee.

EIGHT

SPELLRAISERS

> If the professors of English will complain to me that the students who come to the universities, after all those years of study, still cannot spell friend, I say to them that something's the matter with the way you spell friend.
>
> *Physicist Richard Feynman*

THE SCRIPPS NATIONAL SPELLING Bee is the Superbowl of orthography. It's the time when America's fascination with unusual talent, juvenile superstardom, and immense pressure—Bee-lovers call it "drama"—converge in a swirling tempest of words, etymologies, parts of speech, and orthodontia. For two days, and especially during the live-television broadcast of the final round, spelling is on America's television sets, in its newspapers, and in the minds of its people.

I had never been to the Bee. As a kid, if anyone in my school was tapped to participate in a spelling contest, I certainly never knew about it. Maybe the news was intentionally withheld from students like me, so as not to exacerbate our frustration. Yet over the past decade, excitement over the Bee has exploded, thanks to the combined effect of television cameras, the documentary *Spellbound*, a Broadway musical, and a couple of books and movies. Today, you'd have to live on Mars to escape Bee mania.

The Bee's prominence also provides a unique opportunity for language revolutionaries. For four years now, members of the Simplified Spelling Society have emerged from their hideouts in cyberspace to descend upon the Bee with picket signs. A couple of years ago, the group was stunned by the far-reaching impact of an Associated Press story featuring one of its members and his protest effort. Despite the tongue-in-cheek nature of the article, the Simplifiers quickly realized that working the mainstream media was their ticket to international recognition and increased attention for the spelling reform cause. By attending the Scripps event, they hope to capitalize on the concentration of journalists, many of whom are desperately seeking ways to punch up their Bee reporting. In 2007, the protesters made their strongest showing yet, with almost a dozen people, if you include the hired Ben Franklin look-alike, and me. I wanted to know what modern-day spelling reformers are up against, so when one of them invited me to join the picket line, I accepted.

During our first morning stationed curbside outside the Grand Hyatt Washington, things got off to a rough start. I watched one woman nearly accost a picketer named Elizabeth Kuizenga. "Uh! With global warming, Iraq, and so many other things going on in the world, you mean to tell me you're protesting *spelling*? Ridiculous," she said. The woman was five paces away before Kuizenga could finish her polite reply about how this wasn't actually a protest of the Bee but an "informational picket" about improving literacy. After being snubbed, she looked at me excitedly and said: "Isn't this fun, being an underdog?"

Kuizenga lives in the El Cerrito Hills, not far from Berkeley,

California. Her protest sign pictured a bumble bee and the slogan: "Take the Sting Out of Spelling." Kuizenga is tall, and has blond hair, blue eyes, and an ebullient demeanor. After more than thirty years of teaching English as a second language, the fifty-nine-year-old Kuizenga said she was so fed up with the litany of rule exceptions, homonyms, silent letters, and confusing vowel combinations within English orthography that she decided to do something about it. "Even as a kid," she said, "I thought the spelling system was ridiculous. My mind was just too logical to accept it."

A few minutes later, a bald man wearing a yellow polo shirt paused before entering the hotel and turned to me and a Society member named Peter Boardman. "Go to a library. It's free. If you can't learn to read in America, you can't learn anywhere." Another guy told us that spelling reform was the most absurd thing he had heard of "since they tried to put clothes on horses," and a British television producer said, "Yeah, great idea. Let's just make spelling easy for the stupid people."

Boardman hails from Goton, New York, not far from Ithaca. His car has an Ithaca Hemp Company sticker in the window. He has pale green eyes, a white goatee, and only a few wisps of hair beneath a Panama Jack hat. The last few years, Boardman was forced to miss the DC gathering because of chemotherapy. "They poisoned me. And I was in no condition to object," he said wryly. But this year, nothing was going to keep him from joining his fellow Society members. Hoisting his picket sign—"Let's End the *i* in *Friend*"—he said he put off learning the results of his most recent round of blood tests until after his return. He didn't want the distraction.

While raising nine children and working in special education, Boardman began thinking about spelling reform. He hated all the booby-traps of English orthography, and felt they needlessly made life hard for children. The first place he went looking for more information was the Internet, where he quickly bumped into the Simplified Spelling Society. "At first I thought they were dingbats, which they are. But now they're my people." Boardman is a supporter of a spelling scheme known as "MORE Spelings," which, he explained in an email a few months after the Bee, is "derived from tradishonal spelings withowt regard tu loacal or rejenal acsents," and in which "pronunseashen is a miner consern in the derivashen."

Another member of our platoon was Naill Waldman. Originally from Glasgow, Scotland, Waldman now lives in Ontario, Canada. "Spelling is the bullet hole and illiteracy is the exit wound," he told me. A few years ago, Waldman wrote and self-published a book called *Spelling Dearest*, all about spelling irregularity. The genesis of the book was a seemingly innocuous question from his son: Where do difficult-to-spell words come from? "Dads like to answer their kids' questions. If he'd asked me about just one word, or maybe a question about sex—that would've been easy," said Waldman. Fourteen years later, after burning through his life savings, Waldman finally presented the book to his son. "I was sure it'd be a bestseller," he recalled. As luck would have it, the book was published around the same time as the megahit *Eats, Shoots & Leaves*, and Waldman believes that bad timing did him in. He admits, though, that the thrust of his book may also have hindered its popularity. "People who love a book about old punctuation rules will hate one that's calling for change." It's always harder to fight the power.

Waldman's picket sign featured a head shot of Ronald Reagan and the words: "Sensible Spelling: good enuf for him, good enuf for us." (Reagan used abbreviated spellings from time to time.) Early in the afternoon, a man wearing a stars-and-stripes patterned necktie spotted Waldman's sign and did a double take. Halting his charge down the sidewalk, he gestured to the portrait of the former president and barked at Waldman: "That's insulting. He was a great man." When I later asked Waldman whether he could handle that kind of abuse all weekend long, he laughed. "I'm from fucking Glasgow! I don't let people like that get to me."

I had expected some bewildered and unfriendly reactions from the DC commuter set marching past the hotel. But the truly irate responses were from Bee parents. "We have kids in this event and this is insulting to them and what they've achieved," one mother yelled at Boardman. I can see her point. We were stationed directly outside the building where these families were having one of their most exciting and memorable weekends ever. The Simplified Spelling Society members kept insisting that this was not a protest, that they are fans of the Bee, and that they think the young spelling stars are wonderful. But this attempt at diplomacy fell on deaf ears. Carrying signs with half-cheeky, half-argumentative slogans, we looked like scrooges, raining on a beloved American parade and pooh-poohing the achievements of talented children. Not exactly a stellar PR strategy.

As for the kids, only a few displayed the kind of outward disdain that many adults did; most just looked at us like we were zoo animals. A few came up to ask for buttons, pamphlets, and sometimes to pose for a photograph. One father let his son take a picture, but when Waldman tried to give the boy a button, the father intervened, forbidding the exchange as if Waldman were handing out flyers for a religious cult.

Yet somehow the accumulating criticism and ridicule fueled my comrades' resolve. Alan Campbell, a quiet seventy-seven-year-old man who came all the way from New Zealand, looked undeterred by the heat from passersby or the nearly 100-degree weather. "If we want to get the message out to the world, this is where we need to be," he said. Despite his suppressed immune system, Boardman was similarly impervious. When one man zipped past the two of us without so much as a no-thank-you wave of the hand, and then another guy told us we were promoting "stupidity and ghetto talk," Boardman chuckled: "You'd think his face would splinter if he smiled. The thing is that some people are so traumatized by the experience of learning to spell that they react violently." Call it PTSpD: post-traumatic spelling disorder.

In spite of our perseverance, colorfully decorated posters, and occasional spats with passersby, media interest that first morning was minimal. At one point, Kuizenga did get to debrief two Northwestern University journalism students. When they finished, I asked if they thought the Society members were newsworthy. "Exiting the building to see protesters is probably worth a short something," one of them said. A television reporter from New Zealand disagreed, calling the picketers a bunch of lunatics. Just before lunch, I watched one campaigner engage in what appeared to be a civil conversation with a reporter named Russ Thaler from the Comcast sports network. "[Spelling reform] is something I've never thought of," Thaler told me afterward. "But sadly for the members, it'd cost too much money to change the language—you'd have to rewrite books, change street signs, and the education system . . . But I wouldn't call them *loco*. Sometimes you just have to listen, because people way outside the mainstream may not be totally wrong." But he couldn't file a story. "We cover sports."

Masha Bell is a spelling reformer from Dorset, England, who used to be a schoolteacher. "It's so hard to get media to take this seriously," she said. "It's not like it was in the first part of the twentieth century." Bell spent her early childhood in Lithuania, though you'd never know it from her crisp British accent. She's sixty-two years old, marathoner-fit and, until you get her talking about language, of genteel disposition. "I'm angry. It's just so stupid," she told me. "We waste so much of kids' lives on something so stupid." That something, of course, is English spelling in its current form. Bell and her Society fellows are certain that a better understanding of the twisted history of English orthography, and of the difficulties children face in school as a result of it, will hasten the realization that change is overdue. "If they'd left Chaucer's system intact, English spelling wouldn't be in the mess it's in today," said Bell. Chaucer's spelling or, more likely, the spelling of his scribes, was in fact quite variable, but Bell's more general message is valid: History has wreaked havoc on what used to be a more standard and phonetic orthography.

I asked Bell if she ever thought about abandoning the cause, given the long odds and that people tend to read and write with the language they have, not the language they wish they had. Not at all, Bell said. "It's so defeatist to accept what you've got. Never mind about improving things? It's ridiculous to think that way. We'd still have slavery and women still wouldn't be allowed to vote." The history of progress, she continued, is largely made up of episodes in which people have "tried to improve the lot of the majority. Spelling reform is no different." When she said this, I thought back to the oft-quoted Oxford professor, Max Müller, who told an audience at the 1901 annual meeting of the National Educational Association that practical spelling reformers "should never slumber nor sleep. They should repeat the same thing over and over again, undismayed by indifference, ridicule, contempt, and all the other weapons which the lazy world knows so well how to employ against those who venture to disturb the peace."[1] Then again, that was before society fell head over heels for spelling bees. If English spelling were rewritten into a simpler, more predictable form, what would happen to this treasured pastime?

After hiding my picket sign under one of the broadcast trucks, I rode the three escalators down from the Hyatt lobby and walked into the conference room to listen to a few rounds of the Bee. It was still early in the weekend, which meant easier words like *billiards*, *utterance*, *widower*, and *maniac*. Media people were already swarming. I watched one local television reporter practice her introductory clip for the evening news at least a dozen times. During each take she struggled to lift a copy of *Webster's Unabridged* into the camera's view. A reporter with the *Seattle Times* told me her editor was lukewarm about her proposal for a big, research-driven story on a pending immigration bill. "Then I called to say that I've got these Washington state kids in the Bee and he's like, 'Front page for you!'"

Obedient, factoid, tomorrow. Watching the spellers, I thought back to those years of remedial spelling book shame and the pressure I felt during shotgun word quizzes at the dinner table. Ever since Johnson's dictionary effectively cemented in peoples' minds the right way to spell tens of thousands of words, the ability to spell well has been used as a crude gauge of someone's education and intellect. In 1875, a correspondent for the London *Times*, who was traveling in the United States, reported that spelling bees were an American "infatuation," and that "every town and village is having its 'bee,' attended by crowds who cheer the successful and laugh at those who are afflicted with a 'bad spell.'"[2] But the affliction wasn't written off like a bout of stage fright or briefly bungled arithmetic. Good spelling was—and let's not kid ourselves, still is—seen as a mark of a smart and refined person.

In a letter to his daughter, Thomas Jefferson counseled: "Take care that you never spell a word wrong . . . It produces great praise to a lady to spell well."[3] In a 1750 letter to his son, Lord Chesterfield, one of Britain's highest-ranking officials and an esteemed society man, was similarly concerned: "I must tell you that orthography, in the true sense of the word, is so absolutely necessary for a man of letters, or a gentleman, that one false spelling may fix ridicule upon him for the rest of his life; and I know a man of quality, who never recovered the ridicule of having spelled *wholesome* without the *w*."[4] Jefferson and Chesterfield, I imagine, would not be well suited to greet the Scripps Bee contestants in the "recovery room," which is where they're sent for immediate consolation and psychotherapy after being dinged off the stage.

Spelling as a measure of manners, we know. Spelling as a sign of intelligence, we infer. Think about the last time you read a formal letter with misspellings in it and the unfavorable impression it left behind, not just of carelessness, but also lack of smarts. "Spelling," David Crystal told me, "has become the main diagnostic feature for determining whether someone has been educated in English." People like to judge, and using language is a fabulously convenient way to do so, never mind whether or not it's an accurate measure. "Whereas pronunciation is uneven, vocabulary is always in flux and grammar is problematic," Crystal explained, "spelling shows up in every word and every sentence of our written lives." Fair or not, it has become a proxy for intelligence.

The winner of the 2007 Scripps National Spelling Bee, thirteen-year-old Evan O'Dorney from Danville, California, offered an interesting twist to this conversation. Moments after acing *serrafine* (forceps for clamping a blood vessel), O'Dorney was awkwardly hoisting a trophy with the help of an E. W. Scripps Company rep. The audience erupted in cheers and cameramen circled into position. Then, beneath the blaze of spotlights and flashes, the boy stood next to ABC/ESPN sportscaster Stuart Scott to tell the world what life looks like from inside the winner's circle.

Scott had harmless questions at the ready. He first asked O'Dorney how he spends his time, and whether it's true that he enjoys music and math more than spelling. (Viewers had already learned this about O'Dorney in a brief montage-style profile of the finalists.) The mere mention of these other activities seemed to snap the champion out of a daze and into a happier mindset. "My favorite things to do are math and music," he said. "With the math I really like the way the numbers fit together. And with the music I like to let out ideas by composing notes." Then the buzz-killing blow: "The spelling is just a bunch of memorization."

This response posed a problem for Scott. The window of opportunity for a successful postgame interview is limited. Millions of viewers want something satisfying to button up the rather predictable dramatic arc of the competition, and they want it promptly. Funny, inspired, humbled, charmed—it doesn't really matter, as long as it's from the winner and as long as it's positive. What Scott and the rest of the world got instead was a champion dissing the very contest he had just won. (Talk show host Jimmy Kimmel summed it up a few nights later: "What a slap in the face to the other spellers!")

SCOTT: "Would you like to maybe reassess your likeability of the National Spelling Bee? How do you feel about it now?"

O'DORNEY: "Are you saying I'm supposed to like it more?"

SCOTT: "I'm leaving that up to you. Do you like it more?"

Long pause.

SCOTT: "Maybe, a little bit?"

O'DORNEY, with a placating shrug. "Yeah maybe a little bit."

OVER DINNER AFTER the first day of the Bee, I spoke with Timothy Travis, a sixty-four-year-old Simplified Society Member from King George, Virginia. Working on a glass of red wine, Travis told me that the Society's centennial next year would mark "one hundred years of failure." This dire assessment surprised me because Travis is a dues-paying Society member, because he's here at the Bee, and because earlier in the day he had proven to be the group's most enthusiastic picket-poster maker. "It's really sad," he said. "Reform is just so needed. People are suffering. It's *tragic* how so many kids end up feeling dumb because of spelling."

In Travis's view, history offers precious few moments during which revolutions such as spelling reform can succeed. "Now isn't one of those times," he said. "Will there be another one in the future? I don't know." In some ways he blames himself for having failed to seize a previous window of opportunity. When the *Star Trek* series was at the apex of its popularity, said Travis, he "should have contacted Gene Roddenberry [the show's executive producer] and urged him to have characters in the program use simplified spellings." With Captain Kirk, Spock, Scotty, and the rest of the *Starship Enterprise* crew using these streamlined word forms, viewers would have seen these constructions as futuristic, efficient, and cool. But nowadays, said Travis, he just doesn't see a way for Simplifiers to connect with a public that doesn't seem to care.

For centuries, an essential roadblock to spelling reform has been the absence of a tribunal that could rule on matters of orthography. Equally problematic, though, has been the absence of a uniform voice. In their conviction that the system is unnecessarily difficult and an obstacle to learning, reformers have a common mission. But on the fix itself, they epitomize discord. During one of our meals together, while Bell and Waldman discussed a nuanced point about fifteenth-century orthography, Boardman leaned to me and said: "You realize what they're talking about has nothing to do with spelling reform, right?" A few hours later, Bell pulled me aside in the hotel lobby to let me know that the others in the group "haven't done their homework and don't really get it." Kuizenga likes the RITE spelling system, Boardman is sure the MORE system is the way to go, other campaigners are fans of a letter-trimming protocol called Cut Spelng, and online you can find still more newfangled reform schemes.

But like Melvil Dewey, the Society members have concluded that before they can do anything, they must first build a broader political base. After the first day of protesting, we met in one of the hotel rooms to debrief about what went well and what didn't, and to share the few meager business cards collected from mildly interested reporters. One issue that came up was what to say if a journalist asks how the Society suggests changing the language. "We've got to lie!" shouted Waldman, only half joking about the group's internal discord. The picketers unanimously decided to redouble efforts of evasion. If someone were to ask what words would be changed and how, give a couple of easy examples—*friend* to *frend*, for instance. After that, though, redirect the conversation back to the broader theme of increased awareness about why English spelling hinders literacy and therefore needs changing.

Reinforcements arrived early the next day. One was seventy-seven-year-old Roberta Mahoney from Iowa. A former librarian, Mahoney had recently been contacting all of the 2008 US presidential candidates to tell them about a fail-safe education issue that could attract voters from diverse political backgrounds. (Mahoney has received no response to date.) The other new arrival was Alan Mole, a soft-voiced man from Boulder, Colorado, who, as a former rocket engineer, brings a heavily empirical perspective to the task of reinventing English orthography. With the Ben Franklin look-alike scheduled for early afternoon, things were looking up.

When I found Masha Bell outside the hotel, she was all smiles. "You're witnessing the historic revival of the Simplified Spelling Society," she said. She'd just completed a radio interview with a station based in Birmingham, England, and was scheduled for an interview on *GM Today*, one of Britain's most watched morning shows. Waldman, meanwhile, was charming a Canadian reporter, who had used his Ontario address as a tie-in for a story about the protesters. Despite the heat and continuous vitriol from pissy pedestrians— "You're acting like you're spitting on these kids!"— Waldman stayed upbeat and on message.

A few hours later, Bell hit more pay dirt. *The Times* of London Web site had just posted a piece about the Bee, accompanied by a retrospective about English orthography and a discussion with Bell that didn't make her sound like a wacko. "This is worth its weight in gold," she said. "Better than gold, really." Until that point, Bell had been thinking of skipping the transatlantic trip next year; it's tiring and not cheap. But with this flurry of new interest, she was beginning to have second thoughts.

Then Ben Franklin arrived by taxi. The uncomfortable-looking stockings, tight maroon velvet vest, and eighteenth-century man-blouse made for an impressive costume, but it was the excessive girth, round spectacles, and light waves of unkempt gray hair that convinced me that Franklin impersonator Ralph Archibald is worth every penny of his one thousand dollar fee. Demonstrating media savvy, Archibald decided to plant himself and a few of us protesters on the corner of H and Tenth Streets. That way, we were positioned in the background of cameras across the street. Television crews were already filming teaser segments in advance of the evening news, with the Grand Hyatt as the backdrop. A number of reporters soon noticed the plump Founding Father and the gaggle of protesters, and, following their noses, crossed the street to introduce themselves. At one point I heard Waldman telling a correspondent that we should try to get the United Nations to establish a committee to control English. For a short period of time outside the Hyatt on that May afternoon in 2007, the journalists outnumbered the spelling reformers.

Back in the hotel, the Bee had advanced to the point where the spellers were tackling that class of words preserved in the lexicon for the sole purpose of being dusted off and carted out for national competition. *Trypanosomiasis, vizirial, leucoryx, genizah, ooporphyrin*. The competition room was now packed with families, spellers who had been eliminated, and reporters who looked like they'd had their fill of the Bee. In the hallway, other spellers skittered about, talking about words, watching the competition on a television monitor, and signing each other's Bee programs. One of them was Emma Manning of Pasadena, California, whose parents I'd spoken with earlier.

Manning had been knocked out of the contest when she misspelled *gardez*, a word describing a type of chess move. I asked her mother, Laura, what she thought of the protesters outside. "I think they're charming," she said. "Practical? Maybe not. But we went out to talk with them and they were sweet and supportive of Emma. Just about the nicest protesters I've ever met. And I've been in some protests myself! At some level, though," Manning continued, "they must know that changing the spelling system is impossible. There's no governing body. And with phonetics? I mean, there are just so many varying accents."

Besides, she said, reform might mean the loss of something valuable. Manning says she sees words differently now that she's a Bee parent. She had never thought much about all the other languages that influenced English spelling or the different parts of speech, but as her daughter developed a love of words and started studying for the Bee, Manning found that there was much more to spelling than just remembering what letters go where. "It's those clues and weird little histories that you pick up—that's what makes it interesting."

The week before arriving in Washington, I was in New York City to read through some of Melvil Dewey's old papers in the archives at Columbia University. One night, a friend took me to a famed Harlem jazz club called St. Nick's. It's the kind of place where a legend like Wynton Marsalis might show up unannounced for an impromptu performance. We sat in simple metal chairs at tables with plastic tablecloths, drinking beer and taking in the music. Sometime late in the evening, I thought of straitlaced Dewey. Consumed by a need to make the world more efficient, he probably wouldn't have taken to jazz, with its layered complexity, improvisation, and whimsical journeying.

What Manning said at the Bee helped me put a finger on something I'd only half understood that night at the jazz club. It has to do with the sense of delight she derives from etymology. Spelling, someone once told me, is a palimpsest, which is a piece of parchment that retains remnants or shadows of old words long since erased. It links us to the past. The technical purpose of orthography is merely to give form to words that then convey meaning, not to delight people by illuminating little histories. And yet it does. For all its unevenness and surprises, English spelling is infused with something undeniably appealing. It's jazzy.

But to be honest, while watching the young spellers compete at the 2007 Scripps National Spelling Bee, rarely did I think about the convoluted beauty of English orthography. I mostly just marveled, and wondered what it is about the human brain that makes spelling tougher for some people than for others.

NINE

OF YACHTS AND YETTERSWIPPERS

"It is impossible even to think without a mental picture."
Aristotle

A FEW MONTHS AGO, I described my troubles with spelling to a neuroscientist. He said he thought I might be a "compensated dyslexic," and recommended that I get tested. I had never heard the term, but it was true that in my quest to allocate blame for English spelling difficulty, I had yet to look inward. Biology, it turns out, has much to say about spelling.

I started with a visit to Dr. Uta Frith, a professor of cognitive development at University College London. Almost immediately, she hit me with a spoonerism. A spoonerism is a wordplay that involves swapping corresponding letters or sounds in a set phrase. People sometimes do this by accident when speaking fast because of fatigue or nerves. *Honey, please pick up some stilk at the more* (rather than *milk at the store*)—that type of thing. When the slipup occurs within a word, the technical term is metathesis.* A common way to form spoonerisms is with paired words, like the name of a person, so that Bob Marley becomes Mob Barley. President Hoobert Heever is another one. All of this is familiar to me now, but when I first sat down with Frith to ask if she thought I might be a compensated dyslexic, I'd never heard of a spoonerism.

"Lohn Jennon."

Huh?

"Exactly," she said. "John Lennon. Compensated dyslexics have trouble understanding this." Only then did she explain the game, disregarding my claim that I didn't know what was going on.

"Here's another one. Bemon Lasket."

I tried not to pause, praying that the appropriate synapses in my brain would calculate the correct answer by the time my mouth released that first fateful syllable.

L-l-l . . . emon basket.

"Good," said Frith. "But incredibly slow."

I could feel the blood rising, turning my cheeks bright red.

Give me another.

"Helen Mirren."

Melon Hirren.

"Not bad," she nodded. "But still not fast."

Based on our later discussion of my spelling difficulties as a kid, my slower-than-average reading speed, and my slow spooner-isming, Frith told me that I could be a compensated dyslexic. Her assessment was crude in that she didn't have a chance to give me a formal evaluation; it was more like a reluctant diagnosis at a dinner

---

*Many words in the lexicon have been influenced by this sort of switcheroo, such as the Old English *bridd*, which became *bird*, and *thyrl*, which became *thrill*.

party. Still, my symptoms were so "classic" that she assigned an 80 percent confidence level to her conclusion.

In the 1960s, when Frith came to Britain from Germany, she had to learn English quickly, and did. She married an Englishman, and after only a couple of years in Britain, she was amazed that her husband started asking her how to spell words. He was a terrific reader, which only made his trouble with spelling more perplexing. In contrast, Frith was (and is) a spelling whiz. Confused by this discrepancy, and, more broadly, worried about children falling behind in school, Frith set out to learn more. "Back then, no one wanted to acknowledge that dyslexia even existed," she said. People would say a child is just lazy, has poor eyesight, has parents who don't read to him, or a teacher who's inadequate. "I dismissed all those excuses," said Frith. "In individual cases, yes, these explanations may apply. But not for all children who're having trouble learning to read and write."

Frith sees her prowess with spelling as a deficit in the same way that my (alleged) compensated dyslexia is a deficit. "I'm a clinical case too," she said, describing herself as a "freak of nature." She's adamant that spelling skill has nothing to do with being gifted. "It's a waste of [mental] resources to learn all that spelling if you don't need it," she said. "The fact is you can't help being good or bad at this." Of course one can train hard to get better, but much of this ability is preprogrammed. (I'm not sure I buy Frith's assessment that her spelling prowess is a deficit; it sounds a little like a good-looking person describing what a burden it is to be attractive. But I respect the values-free perspective.)

When it comes to brain function, writing and spelling are essentially subsets of reading. To read, our brains call upon a variety of functions. It isn't a miracle but seems like one because the human brain isn't wired specifically for this task. The evolution of written symbols, words, and prose is far too recent in human history for this operation to be coded into our genes.[1] Instead, the brain has retooled itself for reading and writing, applying, for instance, visual processing powers that evolved for other tasks, possibly functions like cluing in to the facial expressions of others. This retooling also means the reading system is more tenuous than many of us realize. So many components must communicate and perform with absolute precision: auditory and visual operations; language processing, speech control, image storage, and integration of information to build meaning. Reading may be a favorite form of leisure, but for the brain it's no walk in the park.

At any number of links in this fragile chain of operations, things can go awry. The occasional typo, misspelling, misspoken word, stutter, or misreading—those are just hiccups. In other cases, the wiring itself is faulty, and that system error is, in a nutshell, dyslexia. This diagnosis is rendered after alternate explanations—poor teaching, hearing, or vision problems, or perhaps an unsupportive home environment—are all ruled out.

Dyslexia can involve an inability to synthesize text; a deficit in sounding out letters or in storing or recalling words, sounds or meanings; or some combination of these or other limitations. One person may be able to identify all the letters *y-a-c-h-t*, but can't link that string of letters to the sound "yot," even if he knows perfectly well what a yacht is and can say the word in conversation. Someone else who's dyslexic may be unable to divvy up the sound units of a word, so that when she hears *extraordinary*, she can't build syllables from sounds in the divide-and-conquer way that most of us go about learning to read and write. Other people can identify the individual letters in a series, whether it's in a real word like *altitude* or something made up, like *snorbitude*, but can't sound them out. And still other people can read a passage, yet can't think along with the text to digest meaning.

Here are a few things dyslexia isn't. It's not when you write down a phone number and mistakenly flip a couple of digits. It's not when you say *left turn* but mean *right turn*, when you mix up the names of your children, or even when you write an email message riddled with misspellings. Nor is dyslexia simply a mental mirroring that results in backward pictures of letters or words. Dyslexics do sometimes transpose letters, *b* and *d* most notably, but this is a small thread in a more complicated web of difficulties. The frequent association with visual mix-ups traces back to the early days of research into impaired reading, when hypotheses about the roots of dyslexia hinged solely on the visual system.

For the brain, English words come in two types. The first consists of words that can be pieced together by recognizing and producing units of sound. English has forty-four sounds represented by some 1,100 different letter arrangements.[2] When linguists talk about these units, called phonemes, they're not talking about syllables but contrasting sounds, so that "s", "i" and "t" are the three phonemes that comprise the word *sit*. (In the word *van*, the sound unit represented by *v* is different from the sound unit represented by the *f* in *fan* because a *v* is pronounced along with vocal cord vibrations, while an *f* is 'unvoiced.' For other words, phonemes can be represented by more than one letter, such as the *th* in *throw*, which is distinct from the *th* in *these*. And down the rabbit hole we go.) When it comes to reading tens of thousands of English words, the ability to identify and produce these units will get you where you need to go. If you can sound them out, you can write them. *Trunk, basket, reformer, lift, glom, hospital, kernel, sunset, editor.*

This "phonemic awareness" is what young children use to build their early reading and writing skills. Look at the writing of a child between, say, four and eight, and it's peppered with constructions that make perfect phonetic sense to a mind that only builds words by sounding out constituents. *Kik the bal. I luv mi momi. Saly haz appls*—cute stuff that proud parents often post on kitchen refrigerators. When my niece was first beginning to write, she asked me how to spell *Dave*. I told her to give it a try, repeating it back to her extra clearly before I realized that I was hindering more than helping.

For schoolchildren nowadays, education has in many ways caught up with linguistics and brain science. Stern spelling instruction, penalization, and ego-injuring spelling books are, for the most part, a thing of the past. The talk in education today is about "creative" or "invented" spelling. The idea is that during early development of writing skills, correct spelling doesn't matter. Children just need to get comfortable with the manual task of writing out letters and then words. Gradually, the child grows more familiar with the relationships between letters and sounds; that those relationships can be temperamental and inconsistent is a later (and lifelong) lesson. The rest of the theory goes that most children, after encountering a word's correct spelling enough times, will naturally begin using that form of the word, so there's little need to worry about younger years' misspellings. (That is, unless a child is gravely off track, in which case there's a more obvious barrier to learning that needs to be dealt with).

Language skills teachers are, and should be, taking a more evolutionary approach to teaching spelling conventions. One frequently used strategy is to give students a list of new spelling words each week. The words are incorporated into the curriculum in various ways, and then there's a spelling test on Friday. By this time each child has had practice reading, writing and saying the words in varying contexts, so that the quiz at week's end isn't so much a memorization test as it is a way to synthesize recently acquired knowledge. The emphasis is on the word and its meanings, and less so on its physical dimensions.

All of this, however, assumes no major roadblocks to learning. At some point, schoolchildren must face more than sound out-able words because English is also endowed with so many words that fall outside the neat and tidy phonetic orbit. This brings us to the other category of words. English is unlike languages such as Spanish, Dutch, Finnish, Italian, Greek, or German, in which, by and large, what you see is what you get. *Yacht* is a favorite example among researchers. There's no way you can sound it out, and although most people don't remember that day, chances are good that the first time you saw *yacht* you were confused. In this sense, one scientist told me, "English is the most Chinese of the European languages" because our less regular orthography has so many words that are stored as visual data. (Languages like Chinese use symbols that link to associated sound and meaning, as opposed to using symbols to represent sounds that build words. Japanese is a mashup of the two.)

Brains process irregular words differently, and they do so beautifully. The trick is in making an image in our minds of what the irregular word looks like, and tagging that stored image to the pronunciation that goes with it. To read English, every time we encounter words like *yacht, lieutenant, phalanx, mediaeval,* and *quiche*, there's a nanosecond of calculation that takes place, as the brain rifles through a database of stored words and corresponding sounds. Reverse this order for a spelling task, and the process is the same; writing and reading are essentially two sides of the same cognitive coin. Think of the last time you paused to sort out a spelling before typing the word. Perhaps you looked skyward to try to picture the word in your mind, or scribbled possible spellings on scrap paper. The same thing is happening in the heads of those spelling bee whiz kids when they look up at the ceiling or trace imaginary letters on their hands. In this sense, spelling is very much about seeing mental pictures.

The seat of dyslexia is the brain, but it starts with genes. Scientists have known this for decades, thanks in part to studies that reveal strong heritability of reading and writing difficulties, as well as rare cases in which family members show the same unusual deficits, such as the ability to understand the same word when written but not when spoken, or the other way around. By studying dyslexia in different cultures and in twins, researchers are narrowing in on the genetic architecture of the reading system, implicating genes with names like ROBO1 and DYX1C1. As one psychologist explained to me, by identifying the suite of genes needed for proficient reading, we could soon have a way to predict what people will need to help them learn, because we would know precisely which genetic deficiencies trigger which learning disorders.[3]

Still, to say that genes are at the root of something like dyslexia doesn't mean there's a single gene for it that either you inherit it or you don't. That is the case for specific genetic syndromes in which a clearly identified letter error among the billions of letter pairs comprising the genome results in a seriously debilitating disease like hemophilia or sickle-cell anemia. When it comes to behavioral conditions like dyslexia, though, genes are implicated as part of the puzzle, not the single piece that explains the whole. Nevertheless, scientists are confident that genes play a major role predisposing people to a weak link, or links, in the chain of processes required for fluid reading and spelling.[4]

All this talk of biology would suggest that the vicissitudes of a particular orthography don't really matter. One of Uta Frith's recent studies compared the brains of people reading English and Italian.[5] She found that English speakers took more time to begin reading real words and nonsense words—*plig, wost, splonk, flumstery*—than Italians did, presumably because Italians' brains can rely almost exclusively on pronunciation rules, whereas English speakers' brains have to do a bit of additional legwork, determining if a word can be sounded out or needs input from the stored lexicon of irregulars.*

Frith's research suggests that whether or not someone is reading or writing in a language replete with orthographic ambiguities, the patterns of brain function in dyslexics appear to be consistent.†[6] But dyslexia is more prevalent, or at least more easily detectable, in countries where languages like English and French are spoken. These languages act like magnifying glasses, making the condition more noticeable by way of orthographic pitfalls. On the other hand, a trickier orthographic code means milder forms of dyslexia are easier to spot, which is good news for parents and educators. In countries like Italy, Germany, or Finland, trouble with reading can be more easily masked by sticking close to stable phonemic rules.

English orthography doesn't cause or exacerbate dyslexia, yet it does pose challenges where some other orthographies do not. To

---

*Google keeps logs of what searchers are looking for, and comparing the English and Italian versions of search histories, a company programmer told me that while misspelled search terms in Italian are usually caused by typos, misspelled English searches are sometimes caused by typos, of course, but are sometimes the result of someone's difficulty with irregular spellings.

†Patterns of functions may be similar, but a 2008 study by researchers in Hong Kong found that the brains of dyslexic children in Chinese- versus English-speaking cultures may be structurally different.

modern-day spelling reformers, these findings are delicious. Frith and her colleagues did not, and do not, advocate spelling reform. They don't mind, however, saying that their results support, or at least encourage sympathy for, the theoretical argument that altering complex orthographies might help improve literacy.[7]

But before becoming a member of the Simplified Spelling Society or sending your kids to school in Finland, it's worth considering some strong arguments in support of the English spelling code, arguments that contradict the spelling reformers' tenet that English orthography is unnecessarily difficult and that learning it wastes valuable time in school. None other than the high priest of linguistics, Noam Chomsky, has said that English spelling has evolved into "a near optimal system." That sounds bizarre, especially after so many miles and pages spent exploring English spelling's warts and barbs, but the idea is that an orthography that is perfectly reflective of pronunciation may not be ideal. In isolation, words with silent or extra letters may strike people as inefficient, and at times they are. But in other cases, they help our brains draw dotted lines between words with related meanings, such as *sign* and *signature, condemn* and *condemnation, dough* and *doughnut,* or *bomb* and *bombard.* Another benefit to spellings that aren't exclusively geared for pronunciation is that, in the case of the suffix *-ed* for instance, meaning is instantly and uniformly clear, even if the sound of the suffix in the spoken words vary (the *d* sound at the end of the word *showed,* versus the *t* sound at the end of *hiked*).[8]

There is indeed much method to the madness. Upwards of 84 percent of English words are spelled with a predictable lineup of letters—that is, they have logical sound-to-letter correspondence.[9] Add to that tools like a mastery of Latin roots and detailed understanding of parts of speech and etymology, and you're on your way to center stage at the Scripps National Spelling Bee. OK, maybe not, but you're at least dealing with an orthography in which a great many spellings can be easily deduced.

On the other hand, there's no denying that English has traps where some other languages do not, and this can make it extra tough on dyslexics. For someone with a severe form of dyslexia, a seemingly simple spoonerism can be a huge obstacle. With "Helen Mirren," for example, Frith said she sees people who might respond by saying only *melon*. "That's as much of a mountain as they can climb, if they even understand what's being done with the sounds in the first place." The same is often true with other tests. Try this. In the following words, identify the emphasized vowel: *Predicament. Emphasis. Illuminate.* Most people correctly come up with *predica-ment*, *emphasis*, and *illuminate*. But some subjects with dyslexia often have trouble with this task. Others may do fine on this type of sound-based exercise, but have trouble with visual- or memory-dependent tasks, like recalling that the written letter string *yacht* is pronounced "yot."

Compensated dyslexia is essentially a low-grade dyslexia that a person, or rather a person's brain, has found ways to work around, often without the individual knowing it and with little noticeable effect on everyday life. One scientist told me about a lawyer who was a terribly slow reader and probably a compensated dyslexic. How did he ever get through the huge volumes of reading required in law school? By sharpening his skills as a skimmer, not in the sense of cutting corners, but skimming so that he could more rapidly hone in on the essential components of a text and then be sure to read—and process—those portions with added care.

When children are first learning to read and spell, a deficit may be more pronounced, hurting their ability to sound out or piece together words. But with age comes more vocabulary, context, and experience, especially if the home environment is one in which reading is encouraged, all of which can help propel children past what may be early-years-only difficulty. Gradually, a picture of a motorcycle is matched to the letter string that's close to that of *motorcycle*. Gradually, they come to know that a *pint* of ice cream is written like a *mint* candy, even though *pint* and *mint* sound different. Gradually, they come to know through conversation what a yacht is. Months or years later, when they encounter a sentence about rich people doing maritime things, their brains match that word with the proper pronunciation. This is how learning plays out over the course of an orthography education.

A few days after meeting with Frith, I had dinner with an English couple. They are both doctors and one of them teaches at an über-prominent university. (He asked that I not use his name because he worried that his comments were too politically incorrect.) I asked what they thought about compensated dyslexia, before sharing the fact that I may be a case in point. The husband wasted no time: "I think that's basically an excuse of affluence—a diagnosis of convenience for getting more time on exams," he said. Dyslexia, although mysterious, is without question a real thing. But ever-more inclusive diagnoses of mild forms of a condition like dyslexia can, in his view, end up obscuring the real cases. If we're all claiming to be a little OCD, ADHD, dyslexic, and Asperger-y, the people who really need special attention will be drowned out by the overdiagnosed masses.

His wife added that she sees more upper-class parents expressing concern that their children might have a condition like dyslexia or ADHD. Then again, that could be because wealthier families simply have the resources to look into such things, and not necessarily because they're desperate for a diagnosis that will explain away their non-valedictory children. The truth is that the line between disorder and natural variation of brain function is always going to be somewhat blurry. After our dinner, though, I was determined to verify or nullify Frith's back-of-the-envelope diagnosis of my brain with a more detailed analysis of my word-making inner self.

THE EXAMINER AND I sat at a round wooden table in a beige meeting room. I was in San Luis Obispo, California, at the headquarters of Lindamood-Bell Learning Processes. When teachers or parents see that a child is having difficulty learning, whether it's a problem with attention, writing, numbers, comprehension, or what have you, they can turn to a resource like Lindamood-Bell for a more thorough assessment of what's going on in the child's head.

My first task was to read aloud a series of nonsense words: *raff, gat, twem, adjex*. They slowly got tougher: *quiles, cyr, phomocher*—gobbledygook constructions built for the sole purpose, it seemed, of tripping up someone trying to calmly read aloud, which of course is impossible when you know you're being tested for a learning disability.

In the next exercise, I had to hold letter sequences in my mind. The examiner showed me a flashcard that read "htjlf" for four seconds, then hid it and asked me to repeat what I saw. The drill was significantly easier once we moved from consonant-only cards to nonwords that had vowels, constructions like *pregreply* and *recanciously*. Without thinking, I kept muttering the words aloud, as if the action of utterance would give the nonword an in-stereo permanence inside my head.

Next came the colored blocks. After the tester said a series of sounds, I lined up blocks to represent each one, using the same color if I heard the same sound twice. When she said, "Show me 'p', 'i', 'p,'" I lined up three blocks: red, yellow, red. At times it was hard to keep distracting thoughts out of my head, like about how the row of black, yellow, and red blocks made a German flag, but for the most part I did OK on this one.

I finished the day with two spelling tests. The first was only three words long; I had to write out the following nonsense words: *spreft*, *spligrity*, *yetterswipper*. I got all three correct. The fifty-word spelling test was next, and I figured this larger sample would, finally, expose my deficit. Some of the toughest words were: *exaggerate*, *cacophony*, *camouflage*, *malfeasance*, *belligerent*, and *pusillanimous*. I nailed *exaggerate* but botched the others, even though I'd scribbled *belligerent* correctly in the margin when trying to determine what looked right.

I had to wait an hour for my scores to be processed, so for lunch I walked down the hilled driveway from the Lindamood-Bell offices and crossed Higuara Street to Ben Franklin's Sandwiches. Awaiting my order, I flipped open the *Los Angeles Times* and came to a story about researchers who had discovered that the rate at which irregular verbs become regular is mathematically predictable. The past tense of *help* was once *holp*, and the past tense of *chide* was once *chode*. Like so many once-wackier verbs, they have since become regular, forming the past tense by simply tacking on the *-ed* suffix (*helped* and *chided*).[10] Some workhorse verbs, namely *be*, *take*, *have*, and *go* aren't going to be regularized anytime soon. But other irregular verbs, like *wed*, which are used less frequently, might want to get their affairs in order. Irregular verbs are the ancient bones of linguistic rules or trends long since passed, and the only thing compelling us to hold on to them is convention. The same is true of spelling.[11]

ARMS OUTSTRETCHED ACROSS a mess of papers in a sprawling office, Nanci Bell used a pencil to circle my test scores. With shoulder-length brown hair and dressed in a black suit, the director and CEO of Lindamood-Bell looks a little like an academic Jackie Onassis. "I don't see it," said Bell. "Nothing in this test shows that you're a compensated dyslexic. You're fine."

Perplexed, I explained that I'm a horrible speller and if she wanted to, she could inspect the list I've been keeping of words whose spellings continually dog me. Bell just shook her head. "David, I'm sorry. I thought you'd be thrilled. But I just don't see it," she said, looking over her glasses at my test scores once again. "We gave you tons of tests— word attack, the block tests, symbol imagery, spelling—one of those would have shown it," by which she meant the supposed deficit.

We flipped through some of the test papers because I needed to point out mistakes that had caused acute embarrassment during the examination. Look at this, I argued. *Cacophony*: wrong. *Belligerent*: wrong. And although I wanted to burn the paper then and there, I reminded Bell of my inexplicable *camoflague* instead of *camouflage*. "How can you say I'm normal when I'm doing things like that?" I asked. What I meant was: Please don't make me walk out of here without a diagnosis.

Bell didn't budge. "It's about the scores," she said. "Empirical results tell us about what's happening in a brain," more so than any humiliation about certain misspelling. That's the nature of standardized tests, she said with a hint of impatience in her voice. A few weeks after my visit, Bell was slated to be the keynote speaker at the biggest learning-disabilities conference in the country, where the focus is on severe disability: kids who score in the single-digit percentile range on reading tests, and who are falling precariously behind in school. Bell grabbed the page with the three nonsense words: *spref*, *spligrity*, and *yetterswipper*. "Look at this," she said. "Most people don't get all of those. Or the two *g*'s in *exaggerate*—you got that too." But again, she explained, it's not the single episodes of a *beligerent* here or *camoflague* there. It's the percentiles that matter. Statistically speaking, I'm not a bad speller.

It was then that I realized I had fallen victim to one of the most common mistakes there is when it comes to interpreting one's experience in the world: I had confused the anecdotal and the empirical. For decades, I've called myself a bad speller because it seemed like I was one, and because my siblings enjoy reminding me that I am one. Instances of spelling confusion only served to reinforce this image of myself, while so many million correctly spelled words went largely unnoticed, just part of the process of writing.

I now see that I'm quite lucky. One of the cruelest things about dyslexia is the downward spiral effect. If young children have trouble turning letters and letter groups into sounds, they get frustrated with reading and have little motivation to keep doing it. Without reading, and without a word-rich environment, they don't build vocabulary, which is an essential tool for improving other aspects of reading, like guessing meaning and decoding spellings, so they get more frustrated and even less inclined to read, which only sets them further and further back.

Before leaving, Bell said that if I really want to improve my spelling, I should start by taking a few extra moments to hold the picture of words in my mind. I may never become a Scripps Bee champion, but the exercise would help improve my ability to visualize correct spellings.

It was a nice suggestion, but why would I bother investing that kind of time when I have spell-check at my disposal? For poor spellers, dyslexic or otherwise, spell-check is the ultimate compensation tool. Back in London, I had mentioned to Frith that I often hear people lament society's increasing dependence on spell-check, and how technologies like text messaging erode spelling skill. "Ahhh, yes," said Frith. "It's the old view that rote learning of spelling has value and shows one's level of education. I couldn't disagree more."

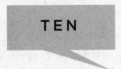
FIXERS

I did wonder, but I didn't want to say anything. I thought to myself: You can fly to Australia via the United States.

German traveler Tobi Gutt. In 2007, Gutt ended up in Sidney, Montana, instead of Sydney, Australia, because of a spelling error while booking his ticket online.[1]

LES EARNEST LIVES IN a woody ranch home in the Silicon Valley hamlet of Los Altos Hills. The house is modest for this part of the country, where it's not unusual for homes to be accented by small vineyards. On a cobalt-sky afternoon in April, Earnest greeted me at the door with a down-to-business hello. He was wearing a gray tie-dyed shirt, loose black pants, and black socks. With a large forehead encroaching on a tiara of gray hair, the grandfather of spell-check looks a bit like Gene Hackman.

We sat in his living room in front of a large metal circular coffee table that hangs from the ceiling by three steel cables. "This is actually the biggest computer disc in the world," said Earnest. "In 1972, we ordered six of them for the lab [at Stanford], but they turned out to be useless." The discs went up for auction, selling for little more than their value as scrap, so Earnest decided to bring one home.

A few months ago, I'd sent out some emails to technology experts, inquiring about the origins of spell-check (*spellcheck*, *spellchecker*, *spelling checker*—take your pick). A winding electronic trail began at the Computer History Museum in San Jose, wove through a few in-boxes at Microsoft, and even mentioned Martha Stewart's boyfriend and one-time International Space Station guest Charles Simonyi. A few weeks later, I received a message from Earnest. "In response to your inquiry, I believe that I created the first spelling checker in 1961."

Spell-check, as you probably know, reviews electronic text for spelling errors and then suggests corrections or makes them automatically. Hundreds of millions of people use the checker within Microsoft Word, and hundreds of millions more are double-checking their words or having them double-checked by similar programs within Apple's operating systems, online tools for blogging and email, or with stand-alone spell-checkers used on open-source platforms like Linux.

With the exception of lexicographers and stalwarts who believe such spelling aids corrupt the mind, most people never give spell-check much thought. If the program gets our attention at all, it's when we curse it for flagging a proper noun, or because it failed to notice that the memo just sent to the boss requests a 10 percent raze. Otherwise, spell-check just quietly runs in the background of our digital lives, much in the same way calculators do. But it too has a story.

Born in San Diego in 1930, Earnest was a mathematics and engineering whiz kid. Like many supersmart teens back then (and now) he ended up in Pasadena at the California Institute of Technology.

In the early 1940s, "all of the electrical engineering people carried slide rules in scabbards on their hips," recalled Earnest. But Earnest chose to arm himself with an abacus, the precursor to the pocket calculator. For greater accuracy, he often performed arithmetic by longhand instead.

In the wake of World War II and the Manhattan Project, scientists were held in the highest regard. Earnest's father was an electronics engineer, and his mother worked on her PhD "in her spare time," eventually becoming a professor at San Diego State University. Earnest was on a similar track, but the Cold War had other plans for him. Looking for ways to avoid the Army draft, he found the Navy's restricted Line Officer program—"the qualifications for which were an engineering degree and poor eyesight"—and eventually ended up at the Naval Air Development Center in Pennsylvania.

The move east marked the beginning of a hopscotching journey between military labs and a stint with the Central Intelligence Agency, all of which Earnest describes as Dr. Strangelove–like inanity interrupted by bursts of exciting computer science. He landed at the Massachusetts Institute of Technology, where he worked on programs with nicknames like Project Whirlwind, Bomarc, and the Semi-Automatic Ground Environment. Some of the projects, like long-range antiaircraft missiles, were the precursors to what today is known as the Star Wars program.

As a computer geek in rooms filled with defense experts, Earnest's responsibilities had nothing to do with military strategy. His role was to work out the equations that became the computational backbone of defense technologies. Doing the math to make these systems operational, said Earnest, gave him a deep understanding of just how flawed they were, so much so that accidental launch wasn't out of the question. "We wrote a paper that we titled: 'Inadvertent

Erection of the Bomarc Missile.' That raised some eyebrows," he said, laughing.

Still, he couldn't deny that for cutting-edge research, a government-funded lab was the place to be. Life as a military scientist also afforded him time to pursue side projects, one of which was a cursive handwriting recognition program that became his masters thesis at MIT. Long before there was such a thing as a desktop computer or a scanner, Earnest was trying to teach a machine to read.

Working with a first-generation computer at MIT's Lincoln Laboratory, he used a special type of pen to write cursive text on the screen, a bit like an Etch A Sketch. From there, the program tried to decipher the different letters, first by seeing if they covered a small area, as with letters like *a*, *n*, *v*, and *c*; whether they were tall, like *b*, *l*, *f*, and *k*; or whether they had a stem—*p*, *g*, *q*, *y*, and *j*. Once the computer had calculated the string of letters, it would return what it "thought" to be the word or words written on the screen.

But a computer can't read without first knowing words and their correct spellings. For the computer to determine if a particular letter was meant to be a cursive *a* or *o*, *g* or *q*, Earnest's program needed a dictionary. So he wrote one. More specifically, he encoded a list of ten thousand correctly spelled words. If the program saw what it calculated to be an *s*, followed by a *p*, followed by a *y*, it could check that letter series against the master list and confirm that this was indeed a word: *spy*.

In the process of trying to match strings of letters to words stored on the master list, Earnest's program often came across things it couldn't identify. Many of those instances were caused by words that weren't in the computer's dictionary. A vocabulary of ten thousand words isn't too impressive: the average high-school graduate has, roughly speaking, a sixty thousand–word vocabulary.[2] Proper nouns also caused problems for Earnest's program, as did sloppy handwriting.

But other times, the trip-up was caused by a misspelling. The letter string *s-p-i* wouldn't have matched anything on the word list, so it would have caused a program error. Earnest had inadvertently built the first spell-checker: A ten thousand–word master list of correctly spelled words, against which other words were compared. (One time, when he wrote out *merry* on the screen, the computer responded with "many, merry" as its possible interpretations. Earnest printed up the *many merry* image and sent it out on that year's Christmas cards.) Earnest's innovation sounds almost prehistoric today, now that we're surrounded by whiz-bang technologies like mobile phones that triple as music players, global positioning systems, and personal digital assistants. But Earnest was working on this nearly fifty years ago. For a computing power reality check, the machine he used for the handwriting recognizer would barely fit on a basketball court.

During my visit, Earnest retrieved from his office what looked like a seven-inch filmstrip reel, but octagonal in shape. A green label read: "L. Earnest," and a blue one read: "Words 7"—the seventh reel of computer tape among the nine that comprise the spelling checker. Gingerly, he took the end of the gray tape and pulled it out of the reel, releasing a microburst of dust. After a couple of feet of blank tape, tiny holes began to appear. Back then, computers were programmed using punched holes on long reels of paper, called tape. Each line of holes is a morsel of data representing either a letter or a space between letters. When people talk about bytes and bits, these patterns of holes are the same thing, but they're punched out in a long sequence of holes instead of being recorded on microchips.

Line up enough dots and spaces and you get a small bundle of information. Bundle those bundles and you get a word, or a sentence. Earnest handed me the reel and it was unexpectedly heavy. The word list that started it all. Sort of.

In 1965, Earnest took a post working at Stanford's Artificial Intelligence Laboratory, and he brought the word list tapes with him. He was already aware, however, of the program's flaws. For one thing, all the words on the original list were in the singular form, which proved problematic when reading plural words. Working with a student researcher, he came up with something called a "suffix stripper," to reduce slipups relating to *y* versus *i-e-s,* for instance. The fix worked well, expanding the list of 10,000 words to several times that number, but it was also a double-edged sword. "If you have *wine, wines,* or *wins,* and you strip the suffix, they all become *win,*" recalled Earnest, which didn't exactly help.

Based on the limited vocabulary it was working with, Earnest's original cursive writing program had an accuracy rate of around 90 percent. The spelling checker developed at Stanford was more successful still. Numbers in the nineties might sound good, and for a baseball hitter or blackjack player, a success rate in excess of, say, 95 percent would be outright astonishing. But for a handwriting recognizer or spell-check program, it's insufficient. Think of it at the sentence level. Every few sentences, another word would be incorrectly corrected or remain incorrect. "If it were interactive you could tolerate higher error rates because you can select right there and then as you go," he said. But in batch mode—when the program goes over the whole text after writing is complete—the high error rate was a killer. Earnest's program had no real-world utility.

Earnest eventually left handwriting recognition and spelling checkers behind. "It did occur to me that a spelling checker of some kind would be useful because my own spelling was atrocious," he said. But he had no way or reason to pursue it, and didn't foresee a personal computer and word-processing revolution coming down the pike. Earnest, who by then had become a lecturer in computer science, moved on to solve other puzzles. A truly useful spelling checker was yet to come, by way of a dictionary controversy in the US and a Communist coup in Czechoslovakia.

TO LEXICOGRAPHERS, THE 1960s are remembered as the decade of the dictionary wars. In 1961, Merriam-Webster published its *Third New International Dictionary, Unabridged*. The editor, Phillip Babcock Gove, figured his job was to record in the dictionary the language as it was used, not how learned men said it should be used. He dared to include entries such as *ain't*, he was less strict about what was considered slang, and he identified, for instance, *biweekly* as meaning both twice a week and every other week. *Flaunt* was defined as an acceptable synonym for *flout*, based on the Merriam-Webster staff's assessment that in American English prose, many writers were using it that way. Gove wasn't out to flaunt conventional definitions. He was a realist. No matter how much some people may loathe the sound or look of *nucular*, *irregardless*, *incentivise*, and *lite*, that doesn't change the fact that other people are bringing these word forms into the language.

Gove's staff at Merriam-Webster brought plenty of prescriptive tradition to the dictionary, and the final product wasn't nearly as renegade as critics suggested. But some entries were more than enough to infuriate language neocons. It turns out that people not only get jumpy when you talk about language change; they even get jumpy when you talk about documenting changes that have already occurred. Critiques soon appeared in *Time*, the *New Yorker*, the *Atlantic*, and other prestigious publications, accusing Gove of failing miserably in his responsibility to uphold a standard of English language correctness.[3]

One person who blew his top over Gove's descriptivism was James Parton, owner of the history magazine *American Heritage*. Outraged by all the same decay-of-the-language laments repeated for centuries, Parton tried to buy out Merriam-Webster. He wanted to put out a new dictionary that would reverse, or at least rein in, Gove's overly inclusive take on acceptable American English. When his takeover failed, Parton contracted with the prestigious publishing firm Houghton Mifflin Company in Boston to launch what would become the *American Heritage Dictionary*.

To begin making a new dictionary, Houghton had to decide what words should be included. This task is complicated. For the *Oxford English Dictionary*, the answer is simple: All of them. That's because the *OED* has adopted a historical approach to language, never jettisoning antiquated words or forms of words. Houghton's people, however, wanted the *American Heritage* to restrict entries, like a Merriam-Webster dictionary does, weeding out words that have gone by the wayside so as to provide a more relevant and finite version of the lexicon.

But what's the best way to take the measure of a language? If you had wanted to glean the most accurate picture of English in, say, the nineteenth century or before, a diligent approach would have been to read Johnson's dictionary and all the works of as many writers as possible, and then spend some time—somewhere between ten months and your entire life—in the streets, playhouses, and taverns of towns wherever English was spoken, carefully listening to words and how they were used. But to take the measure of the language in the modern era, to really capture what it is to the extent that is even possible, digital databases are the way to go.

The publishers at Houghton decided to join forces with pioneers of a nascent discipline that straddled the fields of computer science and linguistics. These experts were applying computing technology and statistics to the study of human language. Modern technologies like in-car navigation systems, translation software, and talking robots are all branches on the computational linguistics tree. So too is spell-check.

Czech-born Henry Kučera was one of the science's trailblazers. After Czechoslovakia's communist coup in 1948, Kučera escaped to the American-occupied zone in Germany. He had nearly completed his PhD in linguistics before fleeing, and was accepted into Harvard as a graduate student in 1949.[4] From there, he became a professor of linguistics at Brown University. In the 1950s, many of Kučera's academic colleagues viewed computers as an oddity, hardly worthy of scholarly pursuit. At that time, Kučera worked on a computer that could store a total of one kilobyte of data. (By comparison, a two-sentence email today takes up about four kilobytes.) But even in those cumbersome early machines, Kučera saw the great potential that computing power could bring to bear on the study of language. Within a decade, he would help propel the worlds of linguistics and lexicography into the Information Age.

Houghton's top brass brought in Kučera to help build a digital version of the language. At Brown, Kučera and his colleagues had already compiled an electronic body of text that lexicographers could use to survey words and their frequency. Compared with the inherently unscientific method of getting a bunch of people to haphazardly mine published material in search of words and meanings, this new approach was revolutionary. For the first time, it was possible to take a statistically rigorous measure of the language.

Houghton, with Kučera's guidance, built a one million–word digital lexicon with short definitions tagged to each entry.[5] Only a piece of the operation was computerized; each word and its spelling was still approved by a one hundred–person panel of language and literature experts, hired to level final judgment about the entries. Nevertheless, the 1969 *American Heritage* was the first dictionary ever to be compiled electronically, and although most consumers probably didn't know or care about the distinction, the technology-based approach gave Houghton an edge over both the *OED* and Merriam-Webster.

By the late '70s and early '80s, when Houghton was already getting ready to publish a second-edition *American Heritage*, a nationwide word-processing bonanza was under way. Companies were racing to design programs for everyday consumers typing on first-generation desktops or stand-alone typewriter-computer hybrids. (When I was in high school, my family owned a Brother-brand word processor with a narrow green screen. My father would watch over my shoulder as I wrote and rewrote sentences, marveling at how easy things had become since he was a kid. Then we would waste ungodly amounts of paper trying to get the machine to print straight across the page.)

Among the emerging breed of word-processing specialists, news spread quickly that Houghton had a digital lexicon. One of the most obvious and, as one Houghton veteran told me, "irresistible," ideas for what to do with the lexicon was to make a spelling verifier. With a list of canonical word forms in the code, any typed string of letters could be compared against the word list, much like Les Earnest's original program, but on a broader scale. If a match didn't show up, the "word" would be flagged as an error or misspelling. Eager to provide this immeasurably useful function to customers, technology firms came to Houghton with checkbooks at the ready. Houghton established a small software division, and in a matter of years had licensed word lists to the likes of Hewlett-Packard, Lang, Digital, Commodore, Sharp, Wang, Panasonic, Sony, Lanier, Brother, and a small Washington-based company called Microsoft.

A huge benefit for the tech companies was that Houghton's word list came with the weight of authority. This wasn't just a list of words thrown together by a bunch of computer geeks. This was a lexicon compiled and confirmed by a group of linguists and literature experts who were using it to produce one of the most authoritative English dictionaries in the world. But having the list wasn't enough. The programmers didn't have the linguistics know-how to write an effective spell-check program. So they came back to Houghton and Kučera asking for help. Within a few years, Houghton's software division introduced spelling correction. Instead of only flagging entries that weren't on the word list, the program could now take those (usually) erroneous entries and run algorithms to calculate words the user had most likely intended to type.

The word lists and checking software were enormously profitable. All of a sudden Houghton, the 150-year-old company that had published the likes of Hawthorne, Thoreau, and Emerson, and was known to most people as an old-school New England publisher of educational texts, had become a tech-sector powerhouse. The company made hundreds of millions of dollars in royalties. Eventually, Houghton executives decided to spin off the software division into a separate company focused on the new horizon of linguistics and computing.

But by the mid-'90s the bottom fell out of the word-processing business, thanks to the ascent of Microsoft. Competing programs faded away, which meant a shrunken market for selling spelling correction software. Then Microsoft decided to buy the technology outright, instead of continuing to pay royalties on every sale of a Microsoft product that contained Houghton's spell-checking goodies. By the time Microsoft had absorbed the word lists and technology that had started with Kučera and the first digital lexicon, spell-check was everywhere.

UBIQUITOUS MAYBE, BUT hardly perfect. Just ask attorney Arthur Dudley. In a brief submitted to San Francisco's First District Court of Appeal in 2006, Dudley accidentally caused some initial confusion, followed by laughter, with the application of the rare legal term *sea sponge*. A similarly shaped term, *sua sponte*, is well-known legalese. It means to act on one's own accord, without prompting from an outside person or entity. But Dudley's word-processing program wasn't up on legal terminology, and the spelling corrector turned *sua sponte* into *sea sponge*.[6]

Still, it's an impressive thing that software can correct, on the fly, so many typos and misspellings. (Adios *seperate*, *ocassionally*, *persaverance*, *liason*, *tendancy*, and *relavent*.) When it comes to the bulk of the work most of us do on computers, spell-check is remarkably helpful. Yet there are a number of reasons why it doesn't always correct correctly. One is that English is just so diverse and continually growing that it's hard to keep updating the word lists to include all the new words, company names and slang in the lexicon.

Another reason why an A+ spelling checker remains elusive is that the natural ways in which humans use language and the variable contexts of speech are extremely complex, so much so that programming a computer to truly understand us has been, is, and will for a long time remain one of the greatest challenges in all of science. One popular spoof on spell-check is an anonymous poem posted on a number of Web sites. It begins:

> *Eye have a spelling chequer,*
> *It came with my Pea Sea.*
> *It plane lee marks four my revue*
> *Miss Steaks I can knot sea.*
> *Eye strike the quays and type a word*
> *And weight four it two say*
> *Weather eye am write oar wrong*
> *It tells me straight a weigh.*

Nevertheless, in-house language experts at places like Microsoft do their best to keep watch over the language and, bit by bit, keep tweaking the word lists and algorithms for suggested correction. Nowadays, countless typos and misspellings get corrected as you type, and new features are moving the programs beyond just canonical forms, flagging, for instance, homophones (*a pear of sox*) and malapropisms (*righteous indigestion*).

Microsoft's language experts also track word requests, as well as frequently corrected "words," to assess whether those words should be added to the Speller dictionary (Speller is the trademark name of Microsoft's spell-checker). One recent request was *pleather*, meaning a plastic faux leather, which was added because of a lobbying effort by the group People for the Ethical Treatment of Animals. If you've got the latest goods from Microsoft, *pleather* shouldn't get a red squiggly.

In other cases, real words are intentionally kept out of the program's dictionary. A *calender* is a machine used for a specialized manufacturing process. But most people see *calender* as a misspelling of *calendar*. More often than not, it is. The wordsmiths at Microsoft have decided to keep *calender* out of the program's dictionary, figuring that at the end of the day it's more useful to fix so many misspelled *calendars*, than it is to cater to the sensibilities of a small subset of the population who happen to know of, and want to write about, *calenders*. Similar homophones (computer people call them "common confusables") include words like *rime*, *kame*, *quire* and *leman*.

Other judgment calls are also embedded in Microsoft's Speller. *Thru* doesn't get the red squiggle, at least on my version of Word, nor does *phone* or *Xmas*. But *X-mas* and *cellphone* get flagged. *Wanna* gets the red squiggle, although most dictionaries say it's an alternative or informal spelling for *want to*. And then there are "words" that fall under the vague category of "restrictions." For a PG–13 example, consider *jackass*. At this moment in spell-check software history, *jackass* isn't going to be called out as a misspelling. It's a word. But type *jakass*, *jackas*, or *jaqueass*, and you'll see the red squiggly three times over, yet without the suggested correction of *jackass*. (You will get, however, *jokes*, *jukes*, *kakas*, *jackals*, and two dozen other suggestions.) *Jackass* is in the Speller's dictionary (i.e., master word list), but presumably as a matter of taste, it has been deemed a restricted word—recognized, but not recommended.

Does this kind of thing have a widespread impact on the language, orthographically or otherwise? Probably not. Even the most enterprising jackass can't come up with that many insults. But this and other wrinkles within the world of spell-check software remind us that behind the curtain of our most authoritative language resources, namely dictionaries and now spell-checkers, are human beings.

* * *

ONE THING THAT never ceases to amaze me about spell-check is that it receives so much flak (or *flack*) from the English-speaking public. People welcome technology into countless areas of their lives. Yet for some reason, they choose to take issue with this particular tool, convinced it's at best harmful, at worst turning our species into slovenly philistines. Bring up the subject of spell-check—or, for that matter, text messaging—in a bar, school, airplane, café, or office park, and you're bound to meet a number of people ready and willing to provide unsolicited sermons asserting that spell-check "is the worst thing ever," "has totally wrecked education," and that "no one can spell anymore because of it." "There's just something very emotional about spelling," a linguist once told me, and it's true. Politics don't seem to matter. Geography doesn't seem to matter, gender doesn't seem to matter, and age seems to matter less than one might think. I meet plenty of twenty- and thirty-somethings who say they can't stand spell-check.

When I visited with Les Earnest at his home in Los Altos Hills, I brought up this common complaint about spell-check. "It's bullshit," he said. "The spelling checker helps teach you to spell. I don't make as many errors now that I use it. And it keeps me straight while also catching typos when I'm typing fast," which he does, working with eight different computers in his home office. But even Earnest isn't a spelling anarchist. "Some people, when emailing, use misspelled words deliberately, to assert informality. Me? I sort of like things to be correct. We should try to spell correctly, just as we should try to do math equations correctly. And I accept spelling checkers as part of the solution."

One day last winter, I dialed Henry Kučera's number in Rhode Island. Now eighty-three years old, he had moved into an assisted-living facility. The telephone rang twice before a man answered with a quavering voice. Introducing myself, I was already sketching in my mind a plan to fly east to meet up with him. We would sit and drink tea together, or maybe a couple of pilsners, and Kučera would tell me about his escape from Czechoslovakia, his love for language, the early days of the wild new science of computational linguistics, and the runaway success of spell-check.

But it wasn't meant to be. "I'm not well," he said. "I can't help you. Not now." From the frailty of his voice, I knew that "not now" meant not ever. The truth is, though, Kučera has already helped me, and millions of other people, every time a spell-check program has whipped a misspelling back into shape before someone who cared could notice. The software is just performing as programmed, but in a small way, we have Kučera to thank every time it happens.

ELEVEN

THE RUBARB ON
THE INTERNET

The waves are beating against the rocky promontory of fixed
spelling all the time.[1]

Lexicographer Robert Burchfield

THE MOST FAMOUS MISSPELLING in business history has got to
be Google. In 1995, two Stanford University graduate students
developed a technique for searching and cataloging Web sites. The
students, Sergey Brin and Larry Page, first called the search engine
BackRub, because the program analyzes the "back links" of Web
sites.[2] Realizing the name wasn't such a hot choice, they sat down with
a few friends to brainstorm a better one. Someone got to thinking of
the dazzling scope of the search operation on an ever-expanding Internet, which led to the idea of names for very large numbers.

Googol is the short version of *googleplex*, which is a 1 followed
by one hundred zeros and is not to be confused with the Russian
writer Nikolai Gogol. The two techies liked the sound of *googol*. A
quick scan for available domain names came up clean: Google.com
was up for grabs. By the time anyone noticed the misspelling, Page

had already registered Google.com, and he and Brin didn't seem to care about the error. They had moved on to other things, stacking computers in Page's dorm room and soon, raising their first twenty-five million dollars in venture capital.

When I arrived on a midsummer afternoon at Google's Mountain View, California, headquarters (also known as the Googleplex), no one was playing beach volleyball in the sand court near the plastic pink flamingos and dinosaur skeleton, but flip-flop-wearing employees were riding commuter bikes between campus buildings; two women were digging in the community organic garden; and clusters of people sat at outdoor tables under sunshades colored yellow, red, blue, or green. Inside one of the campus cafés, a bunch of young Google-ites sat on colored sofas and chairs, sipping lattes and freshly squeezed juices while tapping away on laptops or reading through printouts of code.

I had come to Mountain View to learn about the workings of Google's suggested spelling function, which you may recognize as: "Did you mean: *function*." Peter Norvig, Google's director of research, hurried into the conference room. A white-haired man with wide-open eyes, Norvig wore an ocean-blue Hawaiian shirt, beige shorts, and white sneakers. Before coming to Google in 2002, he was division chief for computational sciences at NASA. He was also a professional speller—once. During a recent Broadway showing of the musical "25th Annual Putnam County Spelling Bee," Norvig volunteered to be an audience participant in the first couple of rounds of the bee. He overstayed his welcome, though, correctly spelling the absurdly difficult words used to send walk-ons back to their seats. The cast eventually had to boot him off stage.

Norvig used to be in charge of Google's search quality program, but his research now focuses on matters of language. A few weeks prior, I'd read an article quoting Norvig as saying there are one hundred trillion words on the Internet. I asked him if that's really true. Norvig shrugged. "You've got to come up with some number," he said, because people like to hear something concrete. "But the real number is infinity. Just hit the 'next' page of your [online] calendar and you've added more words." The more interesting questions, Norvig said, have to do with the millions of unique English words in cyberspace and the novel ways in which people are using them and coining new ones.[3]

You don't need to dig deep into programming code or obscure corners of the Internet to witness this linguistic revolution in action. It starts with a simple search query. According to the company's Web site, Google's spell-check software checks your entry to ensure that you're "using the most common version of a word's spelling. If it calculates that you're likely to generate more relevant search results with an alternative spelling, it will ask 'Did you mean: [more common spelling]?'" For Google-ites responsible for maintaining and improving the search engine, the goal isn't to provide a spell-checking service, although people often use it that way. From a strictly purpose-of-code perspective, Google's spell-check is designed to help you travel as seamlessly as possible through the galaxy of digital information to the site that best matches what your brain is looking for, not what your fingertips might say your brain is looking for. Spelling correction is only a means to that end.

The whole thing works much like a conventional spell-checker, at first. Queries are compared against a giant list of known words, and that list is constantly updated, as new words, pharmaceutical names, celebrities, song lyrics, technical terms, comic-book characters, and advertisements continue piling onto the Web. Google software uses this list to determine whether you might benefit from changing the spelling within your query. Type *seperate*, and even though the search (for me, today) brings up 34.4 million results in 0.14 seconds, Google's results page asks if I meant *separate*, which delivers 280 million search results.

But it's not just *separate*'s presence on a word list or a larger tally of results that tell Google computers to tell me to swap *e* for *a*. The algorithms go deeper than that, and this is where Google search departs, in operation and philosophy, from traditional spell-checkers. It's not about canonical forms. When conducting a search, Google's algorithms don't care about spelling; they care about accurately reflecting what's out there on the Web. Commonly accepted spellings will usually lead a searcher to the desired information. But so too can alternatively spelled or misspelled words.

Although there are other entities in cyberspace named Penny Lane, a search for Penny Lane is, not surprisingly, going to lead first to Web sites about the Beatles song because the most abundant stuff (technically, the most linked-to stuff) regarding Penny Lane relates to the Beatles, not the Wisconsin farm called Penny Lane that makes and sells a southeast Asian sweet and sour dipping sauce.[4] If you search for *peni lane*, you'll still get steered toward the Beatles, but you can also make your way to a page about a New Zealand-based fishing vessel, *Peni Lane*. It all comes down to probabilities, which Norvig and company can build with unprecedented precision because they have an unprecedented amount of data about the language. This year, Google's search engine will perform four hundred billion searches worldwide.[5]

When I enter *rubarb*, Google search redirects me toward the information I want. That may sound scary if you're a technophobe. *Be afraid. Google knows what you're thinking.* But really what we're talking about is one helluva tool. I want information about a certain red and green leafy vegetable. I know it. Google knows it. And there's no point in letting an *h*—a silent one at that—slow my effort to get it.

The last thing Google people want is to be perceived as setting rules or boundaries around what users do. A company as big as Google already has enough trouble dispelling fears of Big Brother-esque practices. "The question, 'Do you mean?' is deliberately ambiguous," said Norvig. "What we're not saying is, 'Here's how you spell.'" In this way, Google can be authoritative without being authoritarian, providing a snapshot of what's out there in cyberspace without presuming to correct your English.

A few years back, Norvig spent a cross-country flight writing what he calls a "toy" spell-checker, to help illustrate what's going on under the hood of Google's suggested spelling function. Outlining one of the program's parameters, he writes: "It would be bad form to say the probability of a word is zero just because we haven't seen it yet." From a mathematical standpoint, this matters tremendously for making the spell-checker as accurate as possible; probabilities of zero have a habit of crashing calculations, so it's easiest to go with a tiny number instead. Yet this computational detail also reflects the linguistic reality of language innovation on the Web. "You never know when things will change," said Norvig. The words *iPhone*, *mashup*, *Skype*, and *kiteboarding* didn't exist until recently. If the code is too doctrinaire in its operation, it will erroneously flag those types of words. *Phone* isn't spelled *i-p-h-o-n-e*. But because of the possibility of something like *iPhone* appearing on the Web, Google's spelling checker has to be inclusive. Or, as Norvig put it: "We let the data decide."

That data is created by the public. When searching for information about a species of dog well known for black-and-white coloring, the majority of humans conducting Google searches type *dalmation*. Google's algorithms don't flag this "misspelling." As one employee put it: "Nobody can spell dalmatian, so neither can we," or more accurately, neither can Google's code. A search for *dalmation* leads directly to the same list of results delivered by a search for *dalmatian*. In one sense, this widening acceptability harkens back to the pre-printing, Haight-Ashbury–style free spelling of Old English manuscripts. Then again, maybe it's not as much a matter of acceptability as it is a shift in how we think about correct and incorrect spelling. As individuals, we may not be conducting our lives with spelling rebellion in mind. Yet cumulatively, we, the wired populace of English users, are asserting control over the orthography of our beloved language, one Internet search at a time.

Launch a search for *airplayn* and Google's program, after calculating that you probably meant *airplane*, will bring up a suggested spelling of *airplane* and a gazillion links to sites with the word spelled correctly. The same goes for *renaisance, kachitori, milennium, accomodation, entreprenur, cematery, floresent*, and countless other common misspellings. Where things start to get interesting is with words that would be considered misspellings to some, but not to others, and not to Google search—words like *dalmation, altho, thru, nite, supercede, int'l, attn, gonna, lemme, wanna, lite, legit, straight-laced*, and *journo* (that's Aussie for *journalist*).

One question that's been nagging me for a while now is whether the members of the Simplified Spelling Society, if armed with the money and technical know-how to put their *enuf, lojic, frend, speling, rime, laking*, and *rubarb* all over the Internet on thousands of pages, might be able to hack the lexicon by forcing their preferred spellings onto so many screens across the planet. "No," said Norvig. "They can't take over common words that are already everywhere." With accepted spellings populating most of interstellar cyberspace, usurping these commonly recognized forms would require a mountain-moving effort that makes spelling reform at the turn of the twentieth century look easy. The Society members might be able to influence some more obscure words, said Norvig, but little beyond that. Even through the Internet, far-reaching language reform by a few, aimed at the many, appears to be impossible.

That doesn't mean, however, that creative spellings sprouting up organically won't take hold and challenge the hegemony of at least a portion of the current standard. The Internet, Crystal had told me, is the one area where a genuine bottom-up alteration of spelling stands a reasonable chance of success in the long term. "You have to ask: Why is a word tough to spell? Because someone once made it difficult. There shouldn't be a *b* in *debt* or an *h* in *rhubarb*. In the past, with print, you could never get away with leaving it out because of copy editors and publishers," he said. "But on the Internet, you can! We're seeing a return to natural, instinctual spelling. This is people voting [for spellings] with their fingertips." Crystal isn't suggesting that these grassroots changes take effect right away, but thirty or fifty years down the road, who knows what might happen? In that sense, the Simplified Spelling Society members should be hopeful. It's not the reform they envisioned—that is, a panel of experts steering the language. But a shake-up is happening, fueled by what looks like an expanding attitude of inclusiveness about words and spelling that has not been seen for centuries.

Blogs, Web sites, chatrooms, email, and text messaging—out on the Web or in our speedy electronic communications, language curmudgeons look more anachronistic by the day. Yet they persevere. In Ireland and the United Kingdom, there have been some recent spats between those who think text message code should be allowed on school papers and tests, and those who vehemently oppose the idea.[6] Online commentary gives the impression that the court of public opinion sides with the view that texting has a poisonous influence on language and literacy.[7] In 2007, Irish education officials concluded that texting erodes students' writing skills. "Text messaging, with its use of phonetic spelling and little or no punctuation, seems to pose a threat to traditional conventions in writing," their report declared. Teens are "unduly reliant on short sentences, simple tenses, and a limited vocabulary."[8] Take that, Hemingway.

Text message code is still too new for long-term rigorous studies of its effect, although Crystal, who recently completed a book about texting, says they are starting to appear and that they suggest texting betters literacy. Negative reports about its impact are generally geared toward a specific—which is to say, stylistic—view of English language skills, not literacy in the developing-brain sense. But since when has sound evidence been a prerequisite for a strong opinion about anything, least of all language? A few years ago, a British Broadcasting Corporation bigwig wrote the following:

> There are so many threats to the survival of good, plain English that it is not easy to be optimistic. Email has a great deal to answer for. Punctuation is no longer required and verbs are abandoned with the speed of a striptease artiste late for her next performance. Text messaging is worse—much worse. Yet I have seen it suggested that students be allowed to use "texting" abbreviations in examinations. Ultimately, no doubt, we shall communicate with a series of grunts—and the evolutionary wheel will have turned full circle.[9]

Really? Consider for a moment this celebrated construction: *OK*. *OK* is a blend of both spelling reform and abbreviation, and took shape long before there was any such thing as the Internet. Although there's some dispute about its exact origin, the leading theory is that it stands for "oll correct" or "ole kurreck," and traces back at least as far as the 1830s, when trendy misspellings and abbreviations were part of the vernacular, such as *NG* for *no go*, *SP* for *small potatoes*, and *GT* for *Gone to Texas*.

Abbreviating and truncating are time-honored traditions not just in English but in languages, period. This trend goes beyond *taxi* from *taxicab*, *bus* from *omnibus*, and *OK* from *oll kurrect*. The likes of *BBQ*, *R & R*, *R & D*, *ASAP*, *TLC*, *PR*, and *FYI* are already well established. And if you're not yet acquainted with *GHGs*, I might as well introduce you to *greenhouse gases*. There's also the slew of corporate- or military-world acronyms and rejiggerings like *MREs*, for *meals ready to eat*, and *reorg* and *recon* for *reorganize* and *reconnaissance*.

Texting is just an extension of truncating and acronymming, whether it's *TBH* (*to be honest*), *FWIW* (*for what it's worth*), *PLOS* (*parents looking over shoulder*), *AIMP* (*always in my prayers*), *ADN* (*any day now*), *AAR8* (*at any rate*), or *4COL* (*for crying out loud*). Ever seen *pwn* for the word "own"? At some point in the recent history of online gaming, someone, somewhere, possessing an ample amount of clout, entered *pwn* instead of *own* (*p* and *o* are keyboard neighbors) in a trash-talking context along the lines of: "I own you this round." The slipped keystroke became a form of insider speak among this networked community of gamers, and then it somehow spread, all the way to the desk of Merriam-Webster dictionary editors.[10] On the Internet, nobody's word concoctions are isolated, and every last one is a candidate for entry into the lexicon, or at least the more welcoming versions of it.

Spend a little time thinking about *OK*, as well as *ASAP*, *FYI*, *AWOL*, *BBQ*, and *SCUBA* (now just *scuba*), not to mention the tried-and-true expression that history repeats itself, and you may find yourself agreeing with Crystal's assessment that the forecast for digital English isn't dire at all. The most devastating blow to traditionalists, aside from the inevitable narrowing of the mind that comes from strict prescriptivism, would be further evidence suggesting that people become *more* sophisticated in their understanding and usage of language, not less, as a result of increasingly digital lives. After all, you have to know what the code stands for. The representation *AAR8* doesn't mean anything to sender or recipient if both don't already know the words and the expression, *at any rate*. Arms crossed in dissent, pundits, if they're not careful, may end up knowing only one thing where others know two—the words and the coded shorthand. Perhaps science will even reveal that the brains of people texting are more active when composing written communications than those who reject it because of some vague notion of correct treatment of English.[11]

Texting is different from spelling, of course, but opinions about it inform the discussion of the future of English orthography. A fundamental question is whether people in cyberspace typing *rubarb*, *altho*, *nite*, *dalmation*, *int'l*, and even *seperate* are categorically wrong. Maybe you feel they are, or that they're so far adrift from convention that they're as good as wrong. If that's the case, you may be pleased to know that while new words and alternative spellings—or maybe it's new "words" and "alternative spellings"—are piling onto the Web, that doesn't mean they're piling unfiltered into some of the more revered records of the lexicon.

At the offices of Merriam-Webster, I asked John Morse about his company's relationship with the forces of the Internet. Although challenging, cyber-catalyzed linguistic evolution doesn't get under Morse's skin. "Google is constantly on any information provider's radar," said Morse. "It's like a giant star coming into your solar system, bending and changing space time." Merriam-Webster staff tries to keep up with the times, introducing features like an online open dictionary, which is essentially Wiktionary without calling it that, and without giving users the keys to the editing kingdom. One recently added word variant: *redonculous*, also *redonkulous*, for *ridiculous*.[12]

From the Merriam-Webster perspective, there are limits to the Internet's usefulness as source material for compiling the contents of a dictionary. When talking about the word *whack*, for instance, Morse said: "We're searching edited prose. That's a lot different than a blog's mention of a rock band called Whack." In Morse's judgment, just because words are on the Web doesn't make them published. A lot of chatroom content, he said, could be likened to the notes kids pass to each other in school, which doesn't pass muster, he said, for dictionary source material.

The general rule at Merriam-Webster is to stay in "protected spaces" online. Yahoo News, Salon, Slate, Boing Boing, and scientific journals on the Web are all safe terrain. But the latest unpaid blogger's posts about country music, a Listserv about caribou hunting or a chatroom devoted to the latest Brazilian pop music? That type of Web content, said Morse, has to be passed over, otherwise we'd end up with "mob rule." Take that, Wikipedia.

I find this view of the lexicon a little redonkulous. First, the flimsiness of the criteria, "edited prose." Surely thousands, if not millions, of well-written blogs and zines that fly under Morse's radar are legitimate sources for new words and meanings, just as an unedited Joyce Carol Oates diary entry, or a back-of-a-napkin essay outline scribbled by Tom Wolfe, are also legit sources. It seems like a huge omission, waving aside this massive volume of words that may be, and most likely is, contributing to language change. That Merriam-Webster embraces mob rule a little with its partially open dictionary, yet applies a different standard to its flagship dictionaries, calls into question the strength—and utility—of modern-day levees upholding language authority.

A more wide-angle view of language in the digital age suggests that the days of the professional word arbiter are numbered, and that some spellings may loosen because of it. Noah Webster's first dictionary was an engine of spelling reform, but there hasn't really been one since. The next revolutionizing force may be the global citizens of English, using what Crystal calls "instinctual spelling." *Milennium, tendancy, reverant, enuf, brocoli, comraderie, privledge, miselanious*—who knows how far it may go, or how far we will let it go? The idea may sound radical, and all together those altered spellings certainly *look* jarring. But the real changes won't be nearly so disruptive—orthographic rebellion that leads to less intelligibility doesn't make much sense. More likely, the process will be natural, almost invisible, like the Great Vowel Shift, or how *goode* became *good, glycerine* became *glycerin, sette* became *set, omnibus* became *bus, catalogue* became *catalog,* and *hiccough* became *hiccup.* But whereas once this process took centuries, it could go much faster on the Web.

Throughout the story of English orthography, attempted reforms (with the exception of Webster's Americanized spellings) have collapsed, in large part because there was no governing body, no *Académie L'Anglaise.* The language, as Benjamin Ide Wheeler told Stanford's Calamity Class of 1906, is the "precious possession of the English-speaking world"—all of us, and most of us share a resistance to anything that smacks of the few telling the many how to behave. It's this populist tradition that adds elements of both hypocrisy and tragedy, I think, to the failed efforts of people like Dewey, today's Simplified Spellers, and other reformers. Many of them held, and hold, power-to-the-people ideals. They want spelling to be easier because they want reading and writing to be easier for everyone. Yet the way they tried to get there was through some sort of orthography oligarchy. No dice.

The criterion of "published material" and "edited prose" used by some present-day lexicographers in their attempts to proscribe the entire language, echo this problem of top-down control. Things aren't nearly as narrow as they once were, back when Samuel Johnson almost single-handedly laid down the laws of English orthography, or when Webster was making himself dizzy with etymologies as he turned circles within his doughnut-shaped desk. Today, Morse's staff can turn to a corpus of text comprised of some one hundred million words. But there're trillions of words in cyberspace, and millions more next week and the week after that. They can't be ignored.

Yet Morse has no option but to limit what his editors read, short of quitting and devoting his energies (without pay) to the growth of Wiktionary. "The largeness of the Web," he said, "makes it impossible. So you sort of have to raise the bar. It's a question of scale. There's just so much electronic text available." It's easy enough for a curious outsider to pester Morse about how lexicographers draw arbitrary lines in the sandscape of the lexicon, but the brave souls on the Merriam-Webster crew still have to put out bound dictionaries. In contrast, the editors of the *OED* have the luxury of just saying yes to everything because the bulk of *OED* editorial energy now goes into *OED Online*, which can grow without limitation. There are still plenty of judgment calls, like which spellings are most common, versus what's slang and what's informal, and how long a word must survive in the vernacular before it earns an official place in the lexicon. But the virtual dictionary has no binding.

Morse, master definer Jim Lowe, and the rest of the Merriam-Webster staff have to stop somewhere—for the collegiate or smaller-sized dictionaries especially, but also for the unabridged edition, which is ironic when you think about the definition of unabridged: "1. not abridged or shortened, as a book. 2. a dictionary that has not been reduced in size by omission of terms or definitions. . . . " Morse tells me that of the tens of thousands of *h*-less *rhubarbs* on the Internet, "if they were all found on message boards written by people who aren't experienced writers, and not appearing anywhere else, then no, I doubt *rubarb* would get in." (On the other hand, all it takes is one US president to use a construction like *nucular* to slingshot it into the realm of officialdom.)

A neologistic and orthographic explosion may be under way in cyberspace, but we still live in a world, for now, in which many people want to buy bound books that contain most of, or at least a terrifically intelligent version of, the English language. Watching me take notes during my visit, Morse nodded toward my notepad. "You'd be nuts not to use shorthand or write *through* as *t-h-r-u* in there," he said. "But as the editor and publisher of a dictionary, I don't have a lot of latitude with creative spellings." Morse must try and lasso every last word, form and meaning, and I suspect that the impossibility of ever completing that task motivates him to conduct his duties with a sense of hyperdelicacy—which of course isn't a real word. Or is it? How would you spell it?

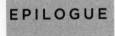

THE PORTLAND
SPELLING BEE

Like any other language, English ultimately reflects the imag-
ination and creativity of those who speak and write it, from
poets and scholars to crooks and beggars.

Robert Clairborne, Our Marvelous Native Tongue.[1]

SPOTLIGHTS MAKE IT HARD not to squint. Before my turn at the
microphone, I fidgeted in my seat, crossing my legs and taking
gulps of beer. Now I'm standing at the front edge of the stage and
there's nothing to do but fold my arms and try to hide the fact that
while others are here for fun, I'm here to exorcise a demon.

The audience quiets and the announcer says my word: *kugel*.

Kugel, I repeat back, the first syllable exploding through the
sound system like a cough. I'm fairly confident I know how to spell
this word, but childhood scars never truly heal. *This is a spelling bee,
for God's sake. Maybe the more manageable first-round words aren't so
easy after all. Am I absolutely positive about* -el *instead of* -le?

I ask for the language of origin, just for the sake of doing it, but
I'm too anxious to process the response. The same goes for an ex-

ample sentence. (For the record: from Yiddish, a baked pudding, served as a side dish or dessert.)

Kugel: *k-u-g-e-l*. Kugel.

That's correct, says the announcer.

Since beginning this project, I have occasionally attended the Monday night spelling bee for adults at a pizza-pub-music-venue near my home in Portland, Oregon. The organizer pulls words from the same word lists used for the National Spelling Bee, but the atmosphere is substantially more relaxed than at Scripps. Participants bring their pints of microbrew on stage, there's a generous intermission for refills and no one seems to mind the occasional hint or mulligan. My MO was to sit in the back, watching, telling myself that this was research. Really, though, I was too nervous to sign up as a contestant. To legitimize the experience, I promised myself that once the book was completed, I would finally step up.

As number fifteen among fifteen participants, I have the advantage of prior attrition, as other spellers fall out of the running. *Lupine, purloin, exigencies, hubristic, oligopsony, navicular.* I make nervous jokes to the woman to my right, admiring her easygoing stage presence. She is a short-haired hipster. When it's her turn to spell, I imagine her launching into a lecture about standard versus correct spelling, about language creativity versus conformity, and about how to reconcile our individual-rights sensibilities with what often appears to be a willingness to bow meekly in response to language experts' declaratives.

Why is it, she asks the crowd, that we accept inventive spelling on Madison Avenue but not on high-school term papers? Lite beer, rite aid, krispy kreme, citibank, sunkist, truvalue, humvee, qwest— sure, they look odd without the capital letters and brand-associated fonts. But they're just words—*our* words—spiced up on behalf of someone else's corporate identity. Fist in the air, the hipster lady says we need to reclaim the orthographic creativity that is rightfully ours.

My next word is *icebound*, a lucky break except that it's accompanied by resentful looks from previously eliminated contestants who drew harder words. I don't rush my reply, but also don't ask for specifics.

Icebound: *i-c-e-b-o-u-n-d*. Icebound.

That's correct, says the announcer, and I return to my seat. *Kilderkin, meiobars, homuncular, dyscalculia.* This last one grabs my attention: "from Latin and Greek, impairment of mathematical ability due to an organic condition of the brain." A slightly frenetic woman wearing a yellow Portland Spelling Bee Champion T-shirt mentions to the audience that she's a grade-school science teacher. She sits down again but in my mind she's halfway into a sermon about how children nowadays are doing horribly in math and science, while every year the emphasis on and adoration of spelling bees continues to intensify. "What's up with that?" she asks.

Scarifier, macrophagous, nephrolithotomy. My next word is *odori*, meaning a type of Japanese dance. When I hear the word it suddenly dawns on me that I might actually win this thing. Because I lived in Japan for a few years, I happen to know that with Japanese words written out in English, what you hear is almost invariably what you get.

Odori: *o-d-o-r-i*. Odori.

With that I'm now one of just five remaining contestants, including the overzealous former champion and two older gentlemen, one of whom sips a drink from a tumbler, and the other a confessed word maniac and former law professor.

In the bee in my brain, the professor speaks lucidly to the crowd:

Why is it, he asks, that so many of us think spell-check and text messaging harm language skills? For centuries people have been whining about English's descent into barbarity, perpetually captivated by this fantasy of a more refined, higher caliber English of bygone eras. I hate to break it to you, class, but English and the spelling code are not in danger.

My final word is *decuman*. An adjective from Latin, it means extremely large or immense, usually in reference to a wave. The sample sentence was: *That decuman wave that took the ship fore and aft swept the life raft off the deck.*

Decuman: *d-e-c-u-m-e-n.* Decuman.

Ding.

Consolation prize (a Tootsie Pop) in hand, I watch the professor triumph over the other three finalists, and in so doing earn a twenty-dollar gift certificate, T-shirt, and bragging rights.

During the early months of my research, I had taken David Crystal's assessment to heart. Maybe I *was* born about one thousand years too late, belonging instead to an age when English had a mostly phonetic and unpoliced spelling code, and no one seemed to mind. But now I'm thinking I was born at just the right time. The Internet and the word-making explosion it has spawned are still so new that the impact on English is only just beginning. Novel challenges to usage authority are already emerging, as more and more people see words not as untouchable objects in a museum, but as clay that they too can shape.

Where's spelling going? My money is on the teens sending text messages and filling up chatrooms with content that most language watchers aren't seeing. They are the new stewards of orthography, tomorrow's "sovereigns over the realms of language." And at the risk of sounding naively optimistic, I don't think that spells trouble.

ACKNOWLEDGMENTS

To everyone in my family: Thank you for your enthusiasm and encouragement.

Thank you, David and Hillary Crystal. You were supportive of this project from the beginning, road trip and all, and I am grateful for your generosity and guidance. For their careful reading and assistance large and small, I
also want to thank my friends, especially Heather Wax, Joshua Davis, Aaron
Earnst, Paul Collins, and Mark Robinson.

I would also like to thank: Howard and Helen Webber, Uta Frith, Guido
Latre, Les Earnest, Win Carus, Henry Kučera, Jack Lynch, Anne Castles, Rawls
Moore, Kate Burridge, and Tom Zeffiro. Alexander Macgillivray, Peter Norvig,
Noah Coccaro and Karen Wickre at Google; Mike Calcagno, Ann Brocken-
brough and Doug Potter at Microsoft; John Morse, Arthur Bicknell, and Jim
Lowe at Merriam-Webster Inc.; Nanci Bell and Gail Phillips at Lindamood-Bell
Learning Centers, and Christopher Dobbs of the Noah Webster House & West
Hartford Historical Society. Masha Bell, Elizabeth Kuizenga, Niall Waldman,
Alan Mole, Peter Boardman, Roberta Mahoney, Timothy Travis, Alan Camp-
bell, and Jack Bovill of the Simplified Spelling Society and American Literacy
Council, as well as Timothy Bates, Jill Lepore, Maria Mody, Rebecca Treiman,
Carolyn Damp, Steven Molinsky and two very smart doctors in England.

Thank you to T. J. Kelleher of Smithsonian Books (now at *Seed* magazine) for a great idea. Thank you Elisabeth Dyssegaard, my editor, and Giles
Anderson, my agent, for taking care of business.

Finally, thank you Nicola. Your love and support are more inspiring
every day.

NOTES

CHAPTER 1: WAR OF THE WORDS

1. His speech was titled simply: *Orthography.*

2. Stanford University and the 1906 Earthquake, http://quake06.stanford.edu/centennial/timeline/index.html

3. Robert Burchfield, *The English Language* (Oxford, England: Oxford University Press, 1985), 147.

4. Monroe E. Deutsch, *Abundant Life: Benjamin Ide Wheeler* (Whitefish, MT: Kessinger Publishing, 2003) (1926).

5. *Chicago Evening Post* July 30, 1913; Melvil Dewey Papers, Rare Books and Manuscript Library, Columbia University Libraries, Box 88.

6. Melvil Dewey Papers, Rare Books and Manuscript Library, Columbia University Libraries, Box 88.

7. George R. Ranow, *American Speech*, Vol. 29, No. 1 (Chapel Hill, NC: Duke University Press, 1954), 36–44.

8. Seth Lerer, *Inventing English* (New York: Columbia University Press, 2007), 22.

CHAPTER 2: CROSSED

1. *From Noah Webster to Merriam-Webster: Celebrating 200 Years of American Dictionary Making* (Springfield, Massachusetts: Merriam-Webster Inc., 2006), 51.

2. Chronology of Events in the History of English, http://www.ruf.rice.edu/~kemmer/Words/chron.html

3. Melvyn Bragg, *The Adventure of English: The Biography of a Language* (New York: Arcade Publishing, 2004), 1.

4. Melvyn Bragg, *The Adventure of English: The Biography of a Language* (New York: Arcade Publishing, 2004), 2; "Chronology of Events in the History of English," http://www.ruf.rice.edu/~kemmer/Words/chron.html

5. *Oxford English Dictionary* entries for *old* and *olde*; Jack Lynch, personal correspondence, April 2008.

6. Medieval Studies at Georgetown University, http://www8.georgetown.edu/departments/medieval/labyrinth/library/oe/texts/a32.2.html

7. David Crystal, *The Stories of English* (Woodstock, New York: The Overlook Press, 2004), 15.

8. Lyrics credited to Naomi Laredo of the Society for Editors and Proofreaders.

9. David Crystal, *The Stories of English* (Woodstock, New York: The Overlook Press, 2004), 54–55.

10. Jean Roemer, *Origins of the English People and the English Language* (New York: D. Appleton & Company, 1888), 352.

11. David Crystal, personal interview, September 2007.

12. Seth Lerer, *Inventing English* (New York: Columbia University Press, 2007), 11.

13. Melvyn Bragg, *The Adventure of English: The Biography of a Language* (New York: Arcade Publishing, 2004), 29.

14. David Crystal, *The Stories of English* (Woodstock, New York: The Overlook Press, 2004), 56.

CHAPTER 3: REGIME CHANGE

1. Melvyn Bragg, *The Adventure of English: The Biography of a Language* (New York: Arcade Publishing, 2004), 32; David Crystal, *The Stories of English* (Woodstock, New York: The Overlook Press, 2004), 145.

2. Melvyn Bragg, *The Adventure of English: The Biography of a Language* (New York: Arcade Publishing, 2004), 35–37.

3. Seth Lerer, *Inventing English* (New York: Columbia University Press, 2007), 63.

4. Melvyn Bragg, *The Adventure of English: The Biography of a Language* (New York: Arcade Publishing, 2004), 54, 60–62.

5. David Crystal, personal interview, September 2007; Vivian Cook, *Accomodating Brocolli in the Cemetary: Or Why Can't Anybody Spell?* (New York: Touchstone, 2004), 12; Henry Alexander, *The Story of Our Language* (New York: Dolphin Books, 1962), 88; David Crystal, *The Fight for English: How Language Pundits Ate, Shot, and Left* (Oxford, England: Oxford University Press, 2006) 26.

6. David Crystal, *The Stories of English* (Woodstock, New York: The Overlook Press, 2004), 150–151.

7. Simon Horobin, "Chaucer's spelling and the manuscripts of *The Canterbury Tales*," ed. Irma Taavitsainen, Terttu Nevalainen, Päivi Pahta, and Matti Rissanen, *Placing Middle English in Context* (New York: Walter de Gruyter, 2000), 202–204.

8. Melvyn Bragg, *The Adventure of English: The Biography of a Language* (New York: Arcade Publishing, 2004), 105; David Crystal personal interview, September 2007.

9. David Crystal, *The Stories of English* (Woodstock, New York: The Overlook Press, 2004), 237.

10. Melvyn Bragg, *The Adventure of English: The Biography of a Language* (New York: Arcade Publishing, 2004), 82.

11. David Crystal, *The Stories of English* (Woodstock, New York: The Overlook Press, 2004), 238.

12. David Crystal, *The Stories of English* (Woodstock, New York: The Overlook Press, 2004), 234.

13. Melvyn Bragg, *The Adventure of English: The Biography of a Language* (New York: Arcade Publishing, 2004), 92.

14. Seth Lerer, *Inventing English* (New York: Columbia University Press, 2007), 118.

15. Seth Lerer, *Inventing English* (New York: Columbia University Press, 2007), 118; David Crystal, *The Stories of English* (Woodstock, New York: The Overlook Press, 2004), 236–237.

CHAPTER 4: PAGE SETUP

1. "A Reasonable Truth: Gore takes off the gloves," *Oregonian*, June 10, 2007.

2. Fran Rees, *Johannes Gutenberg: Inventor of the Printing Press* (Minneapolis: Compass Point Books, 2006), 22.

3. Fran Rees, *Johannes Gutenberg: Inventor of the Printing Press* (Minneapolis: Compass Point Books, 2006), 14.

4. Fran Rees, *Johannes Gutenberg: Inventor of the Printing Press* (Minneapolis: Compass Point Books, 2006), 10.

5. Guido Latre personal interview, September 2007.

6. Robert Burchfield, *The English Language* (Oxford, England: Oxford University Press, 1985), 147.

7. David Crystal, *The Fight for English: How Language Pundits Ate, Shot, and Left* (Oxford, England: Oxford University Press, 2006), 30–31.

8. David Crystal, *The Fight for English: How Language Pundits Ate, Shot, and Left* (Oxford, England: Oxford University Press, 2006), 26.

9. Michael Stubbs, *Language and Literacy: The Sociolinguistics of Reading and Writing* (London: Routledge, 1980), 25.

10. Ron Powers, *Mark Twain: A Life* (New York: Free Press, 2005), 50 [Citing Twain letter to George Bainton dated October 15, 1888]; See also www.twainquotes.com

11. Melvyn Bragg, *The Adventure of English: The Biography of a Language* (New York: Arcade Publishing, 2004), 97.

12. George D. Painter, *William Caxton: A Biography* (New York: G. P. Putnam's Sons, 1976), 22.

13. George D. Painter, *William Caxton: A Biography* (New York: G. P. Putnam's Sons, 1976), 23.

14. George D. Painter, *William Caxton: A Biography* (New York: G. P. Putnam's Sons, 1976), 62–63.

15. George D. Painter, *William Caxton: A Biography* (New York: G. P. Putnam's Sons, 1976), 101.

16. Melvyn Bragg, *The Adventure of English: The Biography of a Language* (New York: Arcade Publishing, 2004), 97.

17. Seth Lerer, *Inventing English* (New York: Columbia University Press, 2007), 99.

18. Melvyn Bragg, *The Adventure of English: The Biography of a Language* (New York: Arcade Publishing, 2004), 97.

19. David Crystal, *The Fight for English: How Language Pundits Ate, Shot, and Left* (Oxford, England: Oxford University Press, 2006), 18.

20. Robert McCrum, Robert MacNeil, and William Cran, *The Story of English* (New York: Penguin, 1986), 87.

21. David Crystal, *The Stories of English* (Woodstock, New York: The Overlook Press, 2004), 258; Robert Burchfield, *The English Language* (Oxford, England: Oxford University Press, 1985), 22.

22. Michael Stubbs, *Language and Literacy: The Sociolinguistics of Reading and Writing* (London: Routledge, 1980), 51.

23. Henry Alexander, *The Story of Our Language* (New York: Dolphin Books, 1962), 89.

24. Melvyn Bragg, *The Adventure of English: The Biography of a Language* (New York: Arcade Publishing, 2004), 89.

CHAPTER 5: VALIANT EXTERMINATORS OF DIALECTICAL VERMIN

1. Melvyn Bragg, *The Adventure of English: The Biography of a Language* (New York: Arcade Publishing, 2004), 120.

2. David Crystal, *The Fight for English: How Language Pundits Ate, Shot, and Left* (Oxford, England: Oxford University Press, 2006), 16.

3. Deborah Cameron, *Verbal Hygiene* (New York: Routledge, 1995), 41–42.

4. Robert McCrum, Robert MacNeil, and William Cran, *The Story of English* (New York: Penguin, 1986), 92.

5. Melvyn Bragg, *The Adventure of English: The Biography of a Language* (New York: Arcade Publishing, 2004), 95.

6. David Crystal, *The Fight for English: How Language Pundits Ate, Shot, and Left* (Oxford, England: Oxford University Press, 2006), 29.

7. Henry Alexander, *The Story of Our Language* (New York: Dolphin Books, 1962), 122.

8. David Crystal, *The Fight for English: How Language Pundits Ate, Shot, and Left* (Oxford, England: Oxford University Press, 2006), 29.

9. *The Concise Oxford Companion to the English Language*, http://www.encyclopedia.com/doc/1O29-B.html

10. Robert McCrum, Robert MacNeil, and William Cran, *The Story of English* (New York: Penguin, 1986), 136.

11. Melvyn Bragg, *The Adventure of English: The Biography of a Language* (New York: Arcade Publishing, 2004), 95.

12. David Crystal personal interview, September 2007.

13. David Crystal, *The Stories of English* (Woodstock, New York: The Overlook Press, 2004), 302.

14. Suzanne Kemmer, "Loanwords: Major Periods of Borrowing in the History of English," http://www.ruf.rice.edu/~kemmer/Words/loanwords.html; David Crystal, *The Stories of English* (Woodstock, New York: The Overlook Press, 2004), 302.

15. Melvyn Bragg, *The Adventure of English: The Biography of a Language* (New York: Arcade Publishing, 2004) 118–119; David Crystal, *The Fight for English: How Language Pundits Ate, Shot, and Left* (Oxford, England: Oxford University Press, 2006), 39, 61.

16. Alexander Gil, as cited in Seth Lerer, *Inventing English* (New York: Columbia University Press, 2007), 148.

17. Oxford University Press computerized survey, http://www.askoxford.com/asktheexperts/faq/aboutenglish/proportion?view=uk; David Crystal personal correspondence, March 2008.

18. David Crystal, *The Fight for English: How Language Pundits Ate, Shot, and Left* (Oxford, England: Oxford University Press, 2006), 28.

19. David Crystal, *The Fight for English: How Language Pundits Ate, Shot, and Left* (Oxford, England: Oxford University Press, 2006), 28.

20. Seth Lerer, *Inventing English* (New York: Columbia University Press, 2007), 115.

21. David Crystal, *The Stories of English* (Woodstock, New York: The Overlook Press, 2004), 268. Also: David Crystal, *The Fight for English: How Language Pundits Ate, Shot, and Left* (Oxford, England: Oxford University Press, 2006), 32.

22. Seth Lerer, *Inventing English* (New York: Columbia University Press, 2007), 161–163.

23. David Crystal, *The Fight for English: How Language Pundits Ate, Shot, and Left* (Oxford, England: Oxford University Press, 2006), 28.

24. David Crystal, *The Stories of English* (Woodstock, New York: The Overlook Press, 2004), 266.

25. Seth Lerer, *Inventing English* (New York: Columbia University Press, 2007), 156.

26. David Crystal, *The Stories of English* (Woodstock, New York: The Overlook Press, 2004), 266.

27. Seth Lerer, *Inventing English* (New York: Columbia University Press, 2007), 160.

28. Bill Bryson, *Made in America: An Informal History of the English Language in the United States* (New York: Perennial, 1994), 15.

29. David Crystal, *The Fight for English: How Language Pundits Ate, Shot, and Left* (Oxford, England: Oxford University Press, 2006), 32.

30. Seth Lerer, *Inventing English* (New York: Columbia University Press, 2007), 156.

31. John Noble Wilford, "World's Languages Dying off Rapidly," *New York Times*, September 18, 2007.

32. Melvyn Bragg, *The Adventure of English: The Biography of a Language* (New York: Arcade Publishing, 2004), 118.

33. Vivian Cook, *Accomodating Brocolli in the Cemetary: Or Why Can't Anybody Spell?* (New York: Touchstone, 2004), 100.

34. Seth Lerer, *Inventing English* (New York: Columbia University Press, 2007), 148.

35. David Crystal, *The Fight for English: How Language Pundits Ate, Shot, and Left* (Oxford, England: Oxford University Press, 2006), 33.

36. British Library Web site scans of Richard Mulcaster, *The Elementarie* (London: Thomas Vautroullier dwelling in the blakfriers by Ludgate, 1582), http://www.21citizen.org.uk/learning/langlit/dic/mul/flinder/mouse.html

37. David Crystal, *The Stories of English* (Woodstock, New York: The Overlook Press, 2004), 269.

38. John Humphrys, Introduction to James Cochrane, *Between You and I: A Little Book of Bad English* (Naperville, Illinois: Sourcebooks Inc., 2004), xiii.

39. David Crystal, *The Fight for English: How Language Pundits Ate, Shot, and Left* (Oxford, England: Oxford University Press, 2006), 68.

40. Melvyn Bragg, *The Adventure of English: The Biography of a Language* (New York: Arcade Publishing, 2004), 197.

41. Robert McCrum, Robert MacNeil, and William Cran, *The Story of English* (New York: Penguin, 1986), 132; Melvyn Bragg, *The Adventure of English: The Biography of a Language* (New York: Arcade Publishing, 2004), 134.

42. Geoffrey Nunberg, *The Way We Talk Now* (Boston: Houghton Mifflin, 2001), 191.

43. James Cochrane, *Between You and I: A Little Book of Bad English* (Naperville, Illinois: Sourcebooks Inc., 2004), 57, 120, 121.

44. David Crystal, personal interview, September 2007; David Crystal, *The Fight for English: How Language Pundits Ate, Shot, and Left* (Oxford, England: Oxford University Press, 2006), 87.

45. Geoffrey Nunberg, *The Way We Talk Now* (Boston: Houghton Mifflin, 2001), 121.

46. David Crystal, *The Fight for English: How Language Pundits Ate, Shot, and Left* (Oxford, England: Oxford University Press, 2006), 217.

47. David Crystal, personal interview, September 2007; David Crystal, *The Fight for English: How Language Pundits Ate, Shot, and Left* (Oxford, England: Oxford University Press, 2006), 168; David Crystal, *The Stories of English* (Woodstock, New York: The Overlook Press, 2004), 477.

48. Charles McGrath, "Death-Knell. Or Death Knell," *New York Times*, October 7, 2007.

49. James Cochrane, *Between You and I: A Little Book of Bad English* (Naperville, Illinois: Sourcebooks Inc., 2004), 121.

50. David Crystal, *The Fight for English: How Language Pundits Ate, Shot, and Left* (Oxford, England: Oxford University Press, 2006), 69.

51. David Crystal, *The Cambridge Encyclopedia of English* (Cambridge, England: Cambridge University Press, 2003), 72.

52. Swift, as cited in Robert McCrum, Robert MacNeil, and William Cran, *The Story of English* (New York: Penguin, 1986), 134.

53. Swift, as cited in David Crystal, *The Fight for English: How Language Pundits Ate, Shot, and Left* (Oxford, England: Oxford University Press, 2006), 71–72.

54. Swift, as cited in Melvyn Bragg, *The Adventure of English: The Biography of a Language* (New York: Arcade Publishing, 2004), 197.

55. John Oldmixon, as cited in Melvyn Bragg, *The Adventure of English: The Biography of a Language* (New York: Arcade Publishing, 2004), 197.

56. Johnson, as cited in David Crystal, *The Fight for English: How Language Pundits Ate, Shot, and Left* (Oxford, England: Oxford University Press, 2006), 73.

57. Jack Lynch, "Johnson's Dictionary Lays Down the Law," The Athenæum of Philadelphia, April 12, 2004, 3.

58. Jack Lynch, "Johnson's Dictionary Lays Down the Law," The Athenæum of Philadelphia, April 12, 2004, 4; Jack Lynch personal interview, May 2007.

59. Jack Lynch, "Johnson's Dictionary Lays Down the Law," The Athenæum of Philadelphia, April 12, 2004, 5. Also Jack Lynch, personal interview, May 2007.

60. Ingrid Tieken-Boon van Ostade and Randy Bax, "Of Dodsley's projects and linguistic influence: The language of Johnson and Lowth," *Historical Sociolinguistics and Sociohistorical Linguistics* Vol. 2, 2002.

61. *Houghton Mifflin Dictionary of Biography* (Boston: Houghton Mifflin, 2003), 814.

62. Jack Lynch, "Review of Kolb & DeMaria, *Johnson on the English Language*," 3. [mailed to author]

63. Jack Lynch, "Reading Johnson's Unreadable Dictionary," Boston Athenæum, January 15, 2004, 2.

CHAPTER 6: OUTLAW ORTHOGRAPHY

1. Henry Gallup Paine, *Handbook of Simplified Spelling* (New York: Simplified Spelling Board, 1920), 16.

2. Isabel Proudfit, *Noah Webster: Father of the Dictionary* (New York: Julian Messner, Inc., 1942), 4.

3. Isabel Proudfit, *Noah Webster: Father of the Dictionary* (New York: Julian Messner, Inc., 1942), 68.

4. Isabel Proudfit, *Noah Webster: Father of the Dictionary* (New York: Julian Messner, Inc., 1942), 18.

5. Isabel Proudfit, *Noah Webster: Father of the Dictionary* (New York: Julian Messner, Inc., 1942), 15.

6. *From Noah Webster to Merriam-Webster: Celebrating 200 Years of American Dictionary Making* (Springfield, Massachusetts: Merriam-Webster Inc., 2006), 11.

7. Jill Lepore, *A is for American: Letters and Other Characters in the Newly United States* (New York: Vintage Books, 2002), 25.

8. Jill Lepore, *A is for American: Letters and Other Characters in the Newly United States* (New York: Vintage Books, 2002), 22.

9. Jill Lepore, *A is for American: Letters and Other Characters in the Newly United States* (New York: Vintage Books, 2002), 22.

10. Seth Lerer, *Inventing English* (New York: Columbia University Press, 2007), 185.

11. Jill Lepore, *A is for American: Letters and Other Characters in the Newly United States* (New York: Vintage Books, 2002), 30, 34.

12. Jill Lepore, *A is for American: Letters and Other Characters in the Newly United States* (New York: Vintage Books, 2002), 31.

13. Jill Lepore, *A is for American: Letters and Other Characters in the Newly United States* (New York: Vintage Books, 2002), 32.

14. Webster, as cited in *From Noah Webster to Merriam-Webster: Celebrating 200 Years of American Dictionary Making* (Springfield, Massachusetts: Merriam-Webster Inc., 2006), 52.

15. David Crystal, *The Fight for English: How Language Pundits Ate, Shot, and Left* (Oxford, England: Oxford University Press, 2006), 268.

16. Isabel Proudfit, *Noah Webster: Father of the Dictionary* (New York: Julian Messner, Inc., 1942), 160.

17. Jill Lepore, *A is for American: Letters and Other Characters in the Newly United States* (New York: Vintage Books, 2002), 30.

18. Jill Lepore, *A is for American: Letters and Other Characters in the Newly United States* (New York: Vintage Books, 2002), 16.

19. Bill Bryson, *Made in America: An Informal History of the English Language in the United States* (New York: Perennial, 1994), 18.

20. Melvyn Bragg, *The Adventure of English: The Biography of a Language* (New York: Arcade Publishing, 2004), 149–154.

21. Jill Lepore, "Noah's Mark," *New Yorker*, November 6, 2006.

22. David Crystal, *The Stories of English* (Woodstock, New York: The Overlook Press, 2004), 421.

23. Lynch talk at National Archives, 1.

24. Jill Lepore, "Noah's Mark," *New Yorker*, November 6, 2006.

25. *From Noah Webster to Merriam-Webster: Celebrating 200 Years of American Dictionary Making* (Springfield, Massachusetts: Merriam-Webster Inc., 2006), 14.

26. Jill Lepore, "Noah's Mark," *New Yorker*, November 2006; *From Noah Webster to Merriam-Webster: Celebrating 200 Years of American Dictionary Making* (Springfield, Massachusetts: Merriam-Webster Inc., 2006), 20.

27. Webster, as cited in *From Noah Webster to Merriam-Webster: Celebrating 200 Years of American Dictionary Making* (Springfield, Massachusetts: Merriam-Webster Inc., 2006), 54.

28. John Morse, personal correspondence, March 2008.

29. Jill Lepore, "Noah's Mark," *New Yorker*, November 6, 2006.

30. Jack Lynch, "Reading Johnson's Unreadable Dictionary," Boston Athenæum, January 15, 2004, 6.

31. Jill Lepore, "Noah's Mark," *New Yorker*, November 6, 2006.

32. Webster, as cited in *From Noah Webster to Merriam-Webster: Celebrating 200 Years of American Dictionary Making* (Springfield, Massachusetts: Merriam-Webster Inc., 2006), 54.

33. Jill Lepore, "Noah's Mark," *New Yorker*, November 6, 2006.

34. Jill Lepore, "Noah's Mark," *New Yorker*, November 6, 2006.

35. Jill Lepore, "Noah's Mark," *New Yorker*, November 6, 2006.

36. Thomas Gustafson, *Representative Words: Politics, Literature, and the American Language, 1776–1865* (Cambridge: Cambridge University Press, 1992), 320.

37. John Morse, personal interview, May 2007.

38. Webster, as cited in *From Noah Webster to Merriam-Webster: Celebrating 200 Years of American Dictionary Making* (Springfield, Massachusetts: Merriam-Webster Inc., 2006), 53.

CHAPTER 7: A FIRST CLASS MAN

1. Melvil Dewey Papers, Rare Books and Manuscript Library, Columbia University Libraries, Box 35A.

2. Melvil Dewey Papers, Rare Books and Manuscript Library, Columbia University Libraries, Box 84.

3. Melvil Dewey Papers, Rare Books and Manuscript Library, Columbia University Libraries, Box 84.

4. Wayne A. Wiegand, *Irrepressible Reformer: A Biography of Melvil Dewey* (Chicago: American Library Association, 1996), 10, 12.

5. Wayne A. Wiegand, *Irrepressible Reformer: A Biography of Melvil Dewey* (Chicago: American Library Association, 1996), 21–22.

6. Letter from Dewey to Vaile dated May 13, 1902. Melvil Dewey Papers, Rare Books and Manuscript Library, Columbia University Libraries, Box 84.

7. Melvil Dewey Papers, Rare Books and Manuscript Library, Columbia University Libraries, Box 85.

8. Bartłomiej Beniowski, *Anti-Absurd or Phrenotypic Alphabet and Orthography for the English Language, Invented by Major Beniowski* (London: Beniowski, 1844), 15, 20.

9. Bartłomiej Beniowski, *Anti-Absurd or Phrenotypic Alphabet and Orthography for the English Language, Invented by Major Beniowski* (London: Beniowski, 1844), 74.

10. David L. Bigler, *Forgotten Kingdom: The Mormon Theocracy in the American West, 1847–1896* (Arthur H. Clark Co., 1998), 56.

11. State of Nevada, Department of Cultural Affairs, Division of Museums and History, "Brigham Young and the Deseret Alphabet," http://dmla.clan.lib.nv.us/docs/museums/reno/thiswas/deseret.htm

12. Brigham Young address, delivered in the Tabernacle, Salt Lake City, October 8, 1868, *Journal of Discourses*, Vol. 12, p. 298, http://www.utlm.org/onlineresources/deseretalphabet.htm

13. State of Nevada, Department of Cultural Affairs, Division of Museums and History, "Brigham Young and the Deseret Alphabet," http://dmla.clan.lib.nv.us/docs/museums/reno/thiswas/deseret.htm

14. Joseph Skibeell, personal correspondence, February 2008.

15. Wayne A. Wiegand, *Irrepressible Reformer: A Biography of Melvil Dewey* (Chicago: American Library Association, 1996), 63.

16. Wayne A. Wiegand, *Irrepressible Reformer: A Biography of Melvil Dewey* (Chicago: American Library Association, 1996), 80–81.

17. Wayne A. Wiegand, *Irrepressible Reformer: A Biography of Melvil Dewey* (Chicago: American Library Association, 1996), 75.

18. Melvil Dewey Papers, Rare Books and Manuscript Library, Columbia University Libraries, Correspondences 1892–1894, S.R.65, Box 84.

19. Funk & Wagnall's letter to Dewey dated November 17, 1890, Melvil Dewey Papers, Rare Books and Manuscript Library, Columbia University Libraries, SS Correspondences 1874–1883, Box 83.

20. Melvil Dewey Papers, Rare Books and Manuscript Library, Columbia University Libraries, Box 84.

21. Melvil Dewey Papers, Rare Books and Manuscript Library, Columbia University Libraries, Box 83.

22. Melvil Dewey Papers, Rare Books and Manuscript Library, Columbia University Libraries, Box 84.

23. Wayne A. Wiegand, *Irrepressible Reformer: A Biography of Melvil Dewey* (Chicago: American Library Association, 1996), 17.

24. Melvil Dewey Papers, Rare Books and Manuscript Library, Columbia University Libraries, Box 84.

25. David Nasaw, *Andrew Carnegie* (New York: The Penguin Press, 2006), 664; Bill Bryson, *The Mother Tongue: English and How It Got That Way* (New York: Perennial, 1990), 130.

26. Henry F. Pringle, *Theodore Roosevelt: A Biography* (New York: Harcourt, Brace & World Inc., 1931), 328.

27. H. W. Brands, *TR: The Last Romantic* (New York: Basic Books, 1997), 566.

28. David Nasaw, *Andrew Carnegie* (New York: The Penguin Press, 2006), 622, 631.

29. "All Federal Printing in the New Spelling." *New York Times*, August 29, 1906.

30. "Children of the Code—Background Research and Notes: Theodore Roosevelt," http://www.childrenofthecode.org/code-history/roosevelt.htm

31. H. W. Brands, *TR: The Last Romantic* (New York: Basic Books, 1997), 566.

32. H. W. Brands, *TR: The Last Romantic* (New York: Basic Books, 1997), 567.

33. *"Roosevelt Spelling Makes Britons Laugh," New York Times* August 26, 1906.

34. H. W. Brands, *TR: The Last Romantic* (New York: Basic Books, 1997), 557.

35. H. W. Brands, *TR: The Last Romantic* (New York: Basic Books, 1997), 557.

36. "Englishmen now call Roosevelt an Autocrat; London Paper Sarcastic About America's Democracy. Spelling Reform by Ukase St. James's Gazette Says President Has Done What Neither King, Czar, Nor Kaiser Could Do," *New York Times*, August 30, 1906.

37. George E. Mowry, *The Era of Theodore Roosevelt: 1900–1912* (New York: HarperCollins College Division, 1968), 212.

38. Henry F. Pringle, *Theodore Roosevelt: A Biography* (New York: Harcourt, Brace & World Inc., 1931), 328.

39. Bill Bryson, *The Mother Tongue: English and How It Got That Way* (New York: Perennial, 1990), 130.

40. "Code Reform Attempts," http://www.childrenofthecode.org/code-history/codereform.htm [video]

41. H. L. Mencken, *The American language: An inquiry into the development of English in the United States*, 2nd Edition (New York: A.A. Knopf, 1921); Bartleby.com, 2000. www.bartleby.com/185/ (accessed April 4, 2008).

42. "Code Reform Attempts," http://www.childrenofthecode.org/code-history/codereform.htm [video]

43. Simon Goodenough, *The Greatest Good Fortune* (Edinburgh: MacDonald, 1985), 223, as cited in David Nasaw, *Andrew Carnegie* (New York: The Penguin Press, 2006), 665.

44. "Code Reform Attempts," http://www.childrenofthecode.org/code-history/codereform.htm [video]

45. Carnegie Collections, Columbia University, Reel 80, letter dated September 29, 1917.

46. Jackson J. Benson, *John Steinbeck, Writer: A Biography* (New York: Penguin, 1990) 155.

47. Bill Bryson, *The Mother Tongue: English and How It Got That Way* (New York: Perennial, 1990), 131; Simplified Spelling Society, "Spelling the *Chicago Tribune* Way, 1934–1975, Part I," http://www.spellingsociety.org/journals/j24/shipley1.php

48. Henry Alexander, *The Story of Our Language* (New York: Dolphin Books, 1962), 31.

49. Stephen Pinker, *The Language Instinct: How the Mind Creates Language* (New York: Harper Perennial, 1994), 188.

50. George Bernard Shaw, Preface to *The Miraculous Birth of Language* (London: Guild Books, 1941) 18.

CHAPTER 8: SPELLRAISERS

1. National Education Association, *Journal of Proceedings and Addresses of the Fortieth Annual Meeting*, University of Chicago Press, 1901, 225.

2. Read, as cited in James Maguire, *American Bee: The National Spelling Bee and the Culture of Word Nerds* (New York: Rodale, 2006), 59.

3. Vivian Cook, *Accomodating Brocolli in the Cemetary: Or Why Can't Anybody Spell?* (New York: Touchstone, 2004), 21.

4. David Crystal, *The Fight for English: How Language Pundits Ate, Shot, and Left* (Oxford, England: Oxford University Press, 2006), 163–164.

CHAPTER 9: OF YACHTS AND YETTERSWIPPERS

1. Maryanne Wolf, *Proust and the Squid: The Story and Science of the Reading Brain* (New York: Harper, 2007) 3, 11.

2. "English a Factor in Dyslexia," Associated Press, March 15, 2001.

3. Timothy Bates, personal interview, March 2007.

4. Anne Castles, personal interview, April 2007; Richard Olson, personal correspondence, June 2007.

5. E. Paulesu, E. McCrory, F. Fazio, L. Menoncello, N. Brunswick, S. F. Cappa, M. Cotelli, G. Cossu, F. Corte, M. Lorusso, S. Pesenti, A. Gallagher, D. Perani, C. Price, C. D. Frith, and U. Frith, A cultural effect on brain function, *Nature Neuroscience* 3(1) (2000), 91–96.

6. W.T. Siok, Z. Niu, Z. Jin, C.A. Perfetti, and L.H. Tan, A Structural-Functional Basis for Dyslexia in the Cortex of Chinese Readers, proceedings of the National Academy of Sciences, online April 7, 2008, 10.1073/PNAS.0801750105

7. E. Paulesu, E. McCrory, F. Fazio, L. Menoncello, N. Brunswick, S. F. Cappa, M. Cotelli, G. Cossu, F. Corte, M. Lorusso, S. Pesenti, A. Gallagher, D. Perani, C. Price, C. D. Frith, and U. Frith, A cultural effect on brain function, *Nature Neuroscience* 3(1) (2000), 91–96.

8. Vivian Cook, *Accomodating Brocolli in the Cemetary: Or Why Can't Anybody Spell?* (New York: Touchstone, 2004), V.

9. Stephen Pinker, *The Language Instinct: How the Mind Creates Language* (New York: Harper Perennial, 1994), 190

10. "How English adds the '-ed,'" *Los Angeles Times*, October 11, 2007.

11. Stephen Pinker, *The Language Instinct: How the Mind Creates Language* (New York: Harper Perennial, 1994), 138.

CHAPTER 10: FIXERS

1. "Spelling mistake takes tourist 13,000km off course," *Register*, January 1, 2007.

2. Stephen Pinker, *The Language Instinct: How the Mind Creates Language* (New York: Harper Perennial, 1994), 150.

3. Herbert C. Morton, *The Story of Webster's Third* (New York: Cambridge University Press, 1994), 1, 7.

4. ed. Benjamin A. Stolz, I. R. Titunik, and Jindřich Toman, *Henry Kučera* (Ann Arbor: Michigan Slavic Publications, 1992), xvii.

5. Howard Webber, "A Brief Account of Spell Checking as Developed by Houghton Mifflin Company," http://www.softwarehistory.org/pdf/X-SpellCheckHM.pdf

6. "Solo's Errant Spell-Check Causes 'Sea Sponge' Invasion," *Recorder*, March 2, 2006.

CHAPTER 11: THE RUBARB ON THE INTERNET

1. Robert Burchfield, *The English Language* (Oxford, England: Oxford University Press, 1985), 147.

2. "From Googol to Google," *Stanford Daily*, February 12, 2003.

3. Google Spokesperson Karen Wikre, personal correspondence, February

2008; Google Research Blog, http://googleresearch.blogspot.com/2006/08/all-our-n-gram-are-belong-to-you.html

4. "Penny Lane Farm LLC," http://www.pennylanefarmsauces.com/

5. Ken Auletta, "The Search Party," *New Yorker*, January 14, 2008.

6. "Exam Chiefs Ridiculed for Allowing 'Text Speak' English Answers," *Daily Mail*, November 1, 2006.

7. "Is txt Ruining the English Language?" *BBC World Have Your Say*, March 3, 2003.

8. "Ireland's Text-Mad Youth Losing Writing Abilities," *USAToday.com*, April, 2007. http://www.usatoday.com/tech/news/2007–04–25-ireland-spells-doom_N.htm.

9. John Humphrys, Introduction to James Cochrane, *Between You and I: A Little Book of Bad English* (Naperville, Illinois: Sourcebooks, Inc., 2005), xxi.

10. John Morse, personal interview, May 2007.

11. "Net Lingo," http://www.netlingo.com/emailsh.cfm

12. "Merriam-Webster Online Open Dictionary," http://www3.merriam-webster.com/opendictionary/newword_display_alpha.php?letter=Re&last=40

EPILOGUE

1. Robert Claiborne, *Our Marvelous Native Tongue* (New York: Three Rivers Press, 1987); Richler, *A Bawdy Language* (Toronto, Canada: Stoddard, 2001), 3.

BIBLIOGRAPHY

Alexander, Henry. *The Story of Our Language.* New York: Dolphin Books, 1962.

Associated Press. "English a Factor in Dyslexia," March 15, 2001.

Associated Press. "Ireland's Text-Mad Youth Losing Writing Abilities," *USA Today. com,* April 25, 2007. http://www.usatoday.com/tech/news/2007-04-25-ireland-spells-doom_N.htm.

Auletta, Ken. "The Search Party." *New Yorker,* January 14, 2008.

Barber, Charles. *The English Language: A Historical Introduction.* Cambridge, U.K.; New York: Cambridge University Press, 1993.

BBC World Have Your Say. "Is txt Ruining the English Language?" March 6, 2003.

Beniowski, Bartłomiej. *Anti-Absurd or Phrenotypic Alphabet and Orthography for the English Language, Invented by Major Beniowski.* London: Beniowski, 1844.

Benson, Jackson J. *John Steinbeck, Writer: A Biography.* New York: Penguin, 1990.

Bigler, David L. *Forgotten Kingdom: The Mormon Theocracy in the American West, 1847-1896.* Spokane, WA: Arthur H. Clark Co., 1998.

Bragg, Melvyn. *The Adventure of English: The Biography of a Language.* New York: Arcade Publishing. Distributed by Time Warner Book Group, 2004.

Brands, H. W. *T. R.: The Last Romantic.* New York: Basic Books, 1997.

Bryson, Bill. *Made in America: An Informal History of the English Language in the United States.* New York: W. Morrow, 1994.

———. *The Mother Tongue: English & How it Got that Way.* New York: W. Morrow, 1990.

Burchfield, Robert. *The English Language.* Oxford, UK, and New York: Oxford University Press, 1985.

Cameron, Deborah. *Verbal Hygiene.* London and New York: Routledge, 1995.

Carnegie Collections, Columbia University.

Children of the Code. http://www.childrenofthecode.org/code-history/roosevelt. htm.

Claiborne, Robert. *Our Marvelous Native Tongue: The Life and Times of the English Language.* New York: Times Books, 1983.

Cochrane, James. *Between You and I: A Little Book of Bad English.* Naperville, Illinois: Sourcebooks, 2005.

Concise Oxford Companion to the English Language. "Topic Page: B" http://www. encyclopedia.com/doc/1029-B.html.

Cook, V. J. *Accomodating Brocolli in the Cemetary: Or Why Can't Anybody Spell?* New York: Simon & Schuster, 2005.

Crystal, David. *The Stories of English.* Woodstock, New York: Overlook Press, 2005.

Crystal, David. *The Fight for English: How Language Pundits Ate, Shot, and Left.* Oxford; New York: Oxford University Press, 2006.

Crystal, David. *The Cambridge Encyclopedia of the English Language.* Cambridge, U.K.; New York: Cambridge University Press, 2003.

"Exam Chiefs Ridiculed for Allowing 'Text Speak' English Answers," *Daily Mail*, November 1, 2006.

Deutsch, Monroe E. *Abundant Life: Benjamin Ide Wheeler (1926)*. Whitefish, Montana: Kessinger Publishing, 2003.

"Englishmen Now Call Roosevelt an Autocrat; London Paper Sarcastic About America's Democracy. Spelling Reform by Ukase St. James's Gazette Says President Has Done What Neither King, Czar, Nor Kaiser Could Do," special cable to the *New York Times*, August 30, 1906.

From Noah Webster to Merriam-Webster: Celebrating 200 Years of American Dictionary Making. Springfield, Massachusetts: Merriam-Webster, 2006.

Goodenough, Simon. *The Greatest Good Fortune: Andrew Carnegie's Gift for Today*. Edinburgh: MacDonald, 1985.

Gustafson, Thomas. *Representative Words: Politics, Literature, and the American Language, 1776-1865*. Cambridge, U.K.; New York: Cambridge University Press, 1992.

Houghton Mifflin Dictionary of Biography. Boston: Houghton Mifflin, 2003.

Kemmer, Suzanne. "Chronology of Events in the History of English," Rice University, http://www.ruf.rice.edu/~kemmer/Words/chron.html.

Lepore, Jill. *A is for American: Letters and Other Characters in the Newly United States*. New York: Alfred A. Knopf, 2002.

Lepore, Jill. "Noah's Mark." *New Yorker*, November 6, 2006.

Lerer, Seth. *Inventing English: A Portable History of the Language*. New York: Columbia University Press, 2007.

Leyden, John. "Spelling Mistake Takes Tourists 13,000 km Off Course," *The Register*, January 1, 2007.

Los Angeles Times, "How English adds the '-ed'," October 11, 2007.

Lynch, Jack. "Reading Johnson's Unreadable Dictionary," Boston Athenæum, January 15, 2004.

Lynch, Jack. "Johnson's Dictionary Lays Down the Law," The Athenæum of Philadelphia, April 12, 2004.

McCrum, Robert, Robert MacNeil and William Cran, *The Story of English*. New York: Penguin Books, 1993.

McGrath, Charles. "Death-Knell. Or Death Knell," *New York Times*, October 7, 2007.

McKee, Mike. "Solo's Errant Spell-Check Causes 'Sea Sponge' Invasion," *The Recorder*, March 2, 2006.

Maguire, James. *American Bee: The National Spelling Bee and the Culture of Word Nerds*. New York: Rodale, 2006.

Melvil Dewey Papers, Rare Books and Manuscript Library, Columbia University Libraries.

Mencken, H.L. *The American language: An inquiry into the development of English in the United States*, 2nd ed. New York: Alfred A. Knopf, 1921; Bartleby.com, 2000. www.bartleby.com/185. [April 4, 2008].

Merriam-Webster Online. Browse Alphabetically: RE. http://www3.merriam-webster.com/opendictionary/newword_display_alpha.php?letter=Re&last=40.

Morton, Herbert C. *The Story of Webster's Third: Phillip Grove's Controversial Dictionary and it's Critics*. Cambridge, U.K.; New York: Cambridge University Press, 1994.

Mowry, George E. *The Era of Theodore Roosevelt: 1900-1912.* New York: Harper, 1958.

Mulcaster, Richard. *The Elementarie.* (London: Thomas Vautroullier dwelling in the blakfriers by Ludgate, 1582).

Nunberg, Geoffrey. *The Way We Talk Now: Commentaries on Language and Culture from NPR's "Fresh Air."* Boston: Houghton Mifflin, 2001.

Nasaw, David. *Andrew Carnegie.* New York: Penguin Press, 2006.

National Education Association. *Journal of Proceedings and Addresses of the Fortieth Annual Meeting.* Chicago: University of Chicago Press, 1901.

Netlingo. "The Largest List of Text Message Shorthand" http://www.netlingo.com/emailsh.cfm/

Paine, Henry Gallup. *Handbook of Simplified Spelling.* New York: Simplified Spelling Board, 1920.

Painter, George D. *William Caxton: A Biography.* New York: Putnam, 1976.

Paulesu, E., et. al., "A Cultural Effect on Brain Function." *Nature Neuroscience* 3 (2001): 91-96.

Penny Lane Farm. http://www.pennylanefarmsauces.com.

Pinker, Stephen. *The Language Instinct: How the Mind Creates Language.* New York: HarperPerennial, 1995.

Powers, Ron. *Mark Twain: A Life.* New York: Free Press, 2005.

Pringle, Henry F. *Theodore Roosevelt: A Biography.* New York: Harcourt, Brace & Company, 1931.

Proudfit, Isabel. *Noah Webster: Father of the Dictionary.* New York: Julian Messner, 1942.

Ranow, George R. *American Speech*, Vol. 29, No. 1. Chapel Hill: Duke University Press, 1954.

"A Reasonable Truth: Gore Takes Off the Gloves," *Oregonian*, June 10, 2007.

Rees, Fran. *Johannes Gutenberg: Inventor of the Printing Press.* Minneapolis: Compass Point Books, 2006.

Sebba, Mark. *Spelling and Society: The Culture and Politics of Orthography Around the World.* Cambridge, U.K.: Cambridge University Press, 2007.

Shaw, George Bernard, preface to *The Miraculous Birth of Language.* New York: Philosophical Library, 1948.

Shipley, John Burke. "Spelling the Chicago Tribune Way, 1934-1975, Part I." from the Spelling Society Web site: http://www.spellingsociety.org/journals/j24/shipley1.php

Hanley, Rachel. "From Googol to Google," *Stanford Daily*, February 12, 2003.

Stanford University and the 1906 Earthquake. Timeline of events: http://quake06.stanford.edu/centennial/timeline/index.html.

State of Nevada, Department of Cultural Affairs, Division of Museums and History, "Brigham Young and the Deseret Alphabet," http://dmla.clan.lib.nv.us/docs/museums/reno/thiswas/deseret.htm.

Stolz, Benjamin A., I. R. Titunik and Jindřich Toman (editors). *For Henry Kučera: Studies in Slavic Philology and Computational Linguistics.* Ann Arbor: Michigan Slavic Publications, 1992.

Stubbs, Michael. *Language and Literacy: The Sociolinguistics of Reading and Writing.* London; Boston: Routledge & Kegan Paul, 1980.

Richler, Howard. *A Bawdy Language: How a Second-Rate Language Slept Its Way to the Top*. Toronto; New York: Stoddart, 1999.

Roemer, Jean. *Origins of the English People and the English Language*. New York: D. Appleton & Company, 1888.

Tieken-Boon van Ostade, Ingrid, and Randy Bax. "Of Dodsley's projects and linguistic influence: The language of Johnson and Lowth." Historical Sociolinguistics and Socio-historical Linguistics, April 2, 2002.

Webber, Howard, "A Brief Account of Spell Checking as Developed by Houghton Mifflin Company," March 2007. http://www.softwarehistory.org/pdf/X-SpellCheckHM.pdf.

Wiegand, Wayne A. *Irrepressible Reformer: A Biography of Melvil Dewey*. Chicago: American Library Association, 1996.

Wilford, John Noble. "World's Languages Dying off Rapidly," *New York Times*, September 18, 2007.

Wolf, Maryanne. *Proust and the Squid: The Story and Science of the Reading Brain*. New York: HarperCollins, 2007.

Young, Brigham. Address, October 8, 1868. From *Journal of Discourses*, Vol. 12.

INDEX